# Education for the New Century

## Views from the Principal's Office

D1231157

*by*
*Donald D. Gainey*
*Principal*

NASSP

Timothy Dyer
**Executive Director**

Thomas Koerner
**Deputy Executive Director**

Kathleen DeFloria
**Associate Executive Director**

Laurel Martin Kanthak
**Associate Executive Director,
Director of Middle Level Education**

Robert Mahaffey
**Director, Editorial Services
and Marketing**

Jackie Rough
**Project Editor**

Eugenia Potter
**Technical Editor**

ISBN 0882102737

## ABOUT THE AUTHOR

Donald Gainey has served as principal of West Warwick High School in Rhode Island for nearly 20 years. He was a member of the NASSP Board of Directors from February 198 to February 1993.

Copyright©1993
National Association of Secondary School Principals
1904 Association Dr., Reston, Va. 22091-1537
(800) 253-7746 • (703) 860-0200

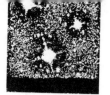

# Contents

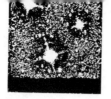

# Foreword

*P*rincipals, assistant principals, and other educators will like this book. I say that unabashedly and without reservation because this is a book that truly reflects the practitioner's point of view.

Not only is *Education for the New Century* written by a principal, it is built upon what many principals have said and are continuing to say about education reform. Described in the author's prologue is the process used in soliciting the thoughts and ideas of practitioners.

Donald Gainey is principal of West Warwick High School in Rhode Island, a position he has held for just about 20 years. In addition, his many years in leadership positions at the state and national levels make him preeminently qualified to write this book. In truth, the merits of this book lie in the author's expertise, his thoughtful judgments, and above all his concern for learning and teaching. He would be the first one to say that education's bottom line in reform is the improvement of learning for all students.

Readers who take a look at this book's contents page — something most readers do in making their decisions about a book's value — will find that the chapters are based on questions, perceptive questions that focus the readers' mind quickly on the points to be made. Donald Gainey, you will see, asks the kinds of questions that are on all our minds. The treat is in reading the discussions, the analyses, and eventually the answers.

We commend this book to your list of "must" reading. We recognize that principals, like all educators, will probably never catch up with all the reading they feel is necessary, but we sincerely hope you will keep this one within reach. You will find it an "easy read" for all the reasons described in this foreword.

Thomas F. Koerner
Deputy Executive Director
NASSP

# *Prologue*

American education has come under intense scrutiny from all segments of society during the past decade. The spiraling national deficit, the national recession, the graying of the American population, the changes in American demography, and the rising need for additional social services to serve our increasingly pluralistic society have created strong competition for the dwindling resources public schools need to fulfill their fundamental purpose of educating *all* students.

Despite these realities and a number of national reports indicating the need for educational reform, the education community has responded by steadfastly maintaining its present course. As an American institution, education appears to have become insular rather than responsive to the changing needs and demands of society. While many educators would take exception to such a statement and point to new programs and technology that have been implemented in different schools, fundamental system-wide changes in the system of education have not occurred. To realize how slow educators are to change, consider how long the education community will continue to operate schools based on an industrial model and an agrarian calendar.

For the past decade, leading educational theorists, policy makers, business leaders, etc. have been extolling the virtues of various plans to reform the educational system. Former President Bush and our nation's governors set forth an agenda for educational reform in terms of national goals for education. Regardless of the specifics of the various plans, most of these individuals have concluded, optimistically or pessimistically depending upon their persuasion, that the public school system in the U.S. is in need of change.

Sifting through the myriad of articles, monographs, books, and reports, a number of common themes have emerged regarding educational reform. Many of these themes include the need for complete restructuring of the system, the need for a new vision and goals to implement the vision, the need for stronger instructional leadership in schools, and the need for a different form of school management. Since the effective schools literature of the late 1970s and 1980s indicated that one common strand was the leadership of the principal, I decided to solicit ideas from principals across the U.S. with regard to educational reform.

To begin this process, I developed an open-ended questionnaire regarding educational reform and sent it to a number of leading principals and administrators in each of the 50 states. Based upon the responses to this questionnaire, a selected number of the initial respondents were asked to complete a follow-up questionnaire. When all the responses to both questionnaires were compiled, most of the respondents indicated that there was indeed a need for change and that practitioners had to play a major role in determining what that change should be.

However, while there was no attempt to quantify the anecdotal comments received in the questionnaires, there was a general consensus of the respondents that some form of reform was in order. Although this sentiment was not universal, there were many questions raised by virtually all the principals. They all seemed to feel constrained, to one degree or another, by the internal and external educational and political systems that would not allow them to reshape and move their schools at a pace to meet the changing needs of the students they serve. Nonetheless, they did express the belief that they could move the reform effort along and make a difference, if given the chance.

Since there was a diversity of responses and suggestions by each of the respondents, this odyssey will be framed around their anecdotal comments and a number of questions, gleaned from their comments, which we will need to respond to as we journey from our present state into the future. These questions will focus on why we have to reform the educational process in our schools, where this reform will take schools as we know them, what educational reform will mean to people, how and when schools and school systems will do what needs to be done, and who will lead this reform. Ultimately, we will have to consider the question of educational reform in the 1990s. Can we get there from here?

Donald D. Gainey
Principal,
West Warwick High School
Rhode Island

# CHAPTER 1

# Why Do Schools Have To Be Reformed?

uring the early '90s, education bashing has become a national, state, and local pastime. Many of the things that people view as being wrong with society are to one degree or another being blamed on the failure of our educational system. The education community, on the other hand, has reacted in a traditional defensive fashion by placing the blame for our present state on society itself. While the finger-pointing rhetoric continues, one of our most precious resources also continues to pass and that is time. A Nation at Risk, which signaled the need for us to question our educational practices, is now a decade old and we still continue to debate educational reform.

Our world has undergone radical changes in recent years. On the home front, the United States went from the greatest economic power in the world to the largest debtor nation in less than a decade. From a global perspective, we have witnessed events of tremendous historical significance, e.g., the reunification of Germany, the fall of communism, the disintegration of the Soviet Union, to cite a few, in just a couple of years. While these inescapable facts represent significant changes in our world, the education community continues to ponder the question of why we have to change. Is there any truth to the observation that if Rip Van Winkle were to awaken today the only place he would feel comfortable would be in a school?

Rather than just responding to these questions out of hand, perhaps it would be beneficial to reflect upon the historical events that have brought us to our present state. Perhaps if we had a clearer vision of why we arrived at our present location, we could more readily address the question of why we must proceed to reform our schools.

> "*It will take looking at how we operate and what we do from a perspective other than that of past experience. What we are doing hasn't changed that much over the years.... We need to look at how we can spend more concentrated time on students who come to school already behind socially and economically. We need to figure out how they learn and how we can teach them.*"
>
> —*A principal*

## Farmers, Laborers, and Clerks

From the dawn of civilization until about 200 years ago, an agrarian society dominated the lives of people around the globe. The family was the productive force for this society. For the most part, the activities of men, women, and children were carried out within and immediately around the household. Those activities most often involved farming; but whether the household was composed of farmers, craftsmen, or merchants, it provided the basis for children to gain the skills they would need to be productive adults. As late as 1810, toward the end of the agrarian age, 87 percent of the population was producing 100 percent of the food needs of the U.S. population. Today, less than 3 percent of the population produces 110 percent of the food needs of the U.S. population, a significant societal change.

Until the mid-1800s, education was intertwined with child rearing as a primary function of the family. Although the Gutenberg press was invented in 1457, the primary source of knowledge was still word-of-mouth, from father and mother to son and daughter, respectively. However, with the advent of common schools, the education of children outside the household began. The primary focus of the early public schools was upon discipline and the three R's, based upon tradition and religious values. Within those early schools, those students who had the will to learn did learn, while those students who did not learn were considered "laggards." This was accept-

> *"An analysis of the implications for education should be done for each of the following: global issues, U.S. and state economic and job issues, changing societies, ethical issues, and changing demographics."*
>
> —A principal

able, since the overall expectation of public education during the agrarian age was a little learning from many students.

This pattern of child rearing and education began to alter as the household began to undergo major changes in the late 19th and early 20th centuries. The production of the individual household was replaced by the "man's" employment in a job outside the home, usually in a factory and more recently an office. The home was no longer the primary source of occupational training for children and became an environment in which only child rearing took place. However, not only did the household relinquish occupational training as a primary function of the family, but it also lost the learning of productive work habits; i.e., the responsibility for completing tasks, punctuality, pride in a craft, etc. As the family became less and less well-equipped to transmit personal characteristics, these functions passed along to the newly founded institution—the public school.

Similarly, the landscape of the U.S. was changing. No longer was America a society of small towns occupied by farmers and shopkeepers, but rather a land of cities, slums, and, later, suburbs occupied by industrialists and factory workers. No longer could schools, designed to serve a rural agrarian society, meet the needs of the urban industrial society that America was becoming. Based in large part upon the work of Frederick Taylor, what the industrial society required was a small cadre of well-educated elites and a mass society trained for semi-skilled or low-skilled jobs. Work was "de-skilled," standardized, and broken down into a series of simple operations that could be repeated in assembly-line fashion. The result was a machine-like work force whose parts could be easily interchanged and/or replaced. Still in its infancy as a major American institution, the public school adapted to the changes in society by adopting a Taylor-like model, which worked well (or so it seemed) in an industrialized society, as the basis for educating children.

Thus, the purpose of the schools shifted from an emphasis on providing a basic education to promote a common culture to the selection and sorting of students in a way that would meet the needs of an industrialized society. In those days, few educators believed that every student could learn. Rather, based upon early studies of intelligence that equated aptitude with the capacity to learn and the notion that aptitude was normally distributed, some students were considered good learners, and others poor learners. Since students differed in their capacity to learn, however, much learning was expected from some students, while little was expected of others. While the lack of learning by some students was deplored, it was acceptable in the free-market system of the industrial society. In essence, each student was presented with the opportunity to learn or to fail.

As the industrial society eclipsed the agrarian society, another trend that

> "*The deterioration of the family unit and the increase of working mothers has created unsupervised situations in the home which must be dealt with as part of the solution to improve our schools.*"
>
> —*A principal*

began to occur in the American household and family had important implications for the school. Women began leaving the household to enter the paid labor market. While this trend continues today, it also necessitates an increasing shift in the child rearing responsibilities from the household and the family to other newly created institutions and schools. With both parents working outside the home, it has become more difficult for the family to reinforce in their children those personal characteristics and values that would promote good performance in school. Ironically, those factors and others, which had only recently been delegated to schools, placed an additional burden on the schools at the very time society was demanding more of them.

In 1956, few people paid attention to a fact that would have dire consequences on society today. For the first time in American history, white-collar workers outnumbered blue-collar workers. The industrial society was giving way to a new society where most Americans worked with information rather than producing goods. This transition from an industrial society to an information society, while still not fully understood nor accepted by policy makers and the general public, has occurred with unprecedented speed.

While the agrarian society lasted for a millennium, the industrial society in the U.S., from its infancy to its demise, lasted for little more than a century. Furthermore, while the transition from an agrarian society to an industrial society could be measured in arithmetic terms, the transition from an industrial society to an information society needs to be measured exponentially. It has been estimated that if the amount of information humanity possessed in the 14th century would fit into a wheelbarrow, what is known today would barely fit into the Grand Canyon; that more new information has been produced in the last 30 years than in the previous 5,000; that the amount of available information now doubles every 5 years; and that by the turn of the century the time it will take for information to double will be every 20 months. The implications of these facts for education have been profound, as has the research conducted on education itself.

Based upon the effective schools research, studies have shown that aptitude predicts the rate of learning rather than the level or complexity of learning. Therefore, since all students can learn given sufficient time and the proper assistance, the industrial society's notion of good and poor learners is slowly giving way to the information society's concept of fast and slow learners. The resulting expectation is that much learning is expected from all students.

In turn, there is an obligation for schools to teach all students, rather than just providing students with an opportunity to learn. However, just as the new realities of the information age are being comprehended by society, so too is the reality that schools can no longer accept non-learning by any student if American society is to remain competitive in the global society produced by the information age.

> "*Students must be taught how to engage in higher order thinking, must realize the interrelationship of all subject matter, must develop problem solving skills, and must acquire knowledge and skills needed to learn effectively, no matter what the learning situation is, so that they will be prepared for a world that is in constant change. Their success will determine our future success as a nation.*"
>
> —*A principal*

## Possessions, Money, and Brains

To illustrate this latter point, again it might be helpful to reflect upon the factors that led us to our present state. During the agrarian age, a typical family's power and wealth were measured by its possessions, i.e., land, livestock, gold, etc. These possessions were tangible and durable commodities. In such a society, there was little need for a formal education in the three R's since the transmission of skills needed for a productive adult life was a function of the family.

However, as we progressed from an agrarian society to an industrial society those economic standards also changed. Our rapid growth as a nation and as an industrial power was based on a number of factors which the U.S. was fortunate to possess. America was a land rich in raw materials with a growing population of semi-skilled and unskilled laborers. The great "melting pot" of the American population was fueled by a growing immigrant population. Possessing an industrious work ethic, those individuals were willing to forsake the intimacy of their cultural diversity to assume a new public identity in a new land

and ultimately formed the relatively homogeneous middle class of the mass society. Furthermore, the contiguous landmass of the U.S. supported mass production, mass marketing, and mass distribution of goods.

One major by-product of this new industrial society was a change in the economic basis of the new society. With the growth of the new society, tangible possessions gave way to paper money as a symbol of the industrial family's power and wealth. This symbolic transformation for the basis of the new economy produced a need that the family was not prepared to fulfill—a population literate in the basic skills of the three R's. Hence, the newly formed institution of the public school was able to provide a service to meet the needs of a mass society by educating America's youth to be productive members of the growing republic.

As the industrial society continued to grow, so too did the diversity of new industries. Yet, the underlying principles of the industrial society were control and standardization. The elite industrial managers and factory workers, the masses, operated in different spheres of influence. Managers did the thinking. Their primary responsibilities included breaking down each job into a finite set of tasks; attempting to find the one best way to complete the task; matching workers to the task; and, supervising, rewarding, and punishing workers.

On the other hand, the responsibilities of the worker were primarily to be trained how to perform specific tasks set forth by "his" immediate supervisor

*"Focus on the process of learning rather than content. It will be the key to the future."*

*—A principal*

in a particular manner, to perform those tasks in a repetitive manner, and to meet quotas in a reliable and predictable manner. In essence, the worker was not required nor encouraged to think, "he" merely did what "he" was told. While the great mass of workers labored in relatively low-skilled jobs requiring little training, their reward for meeting the expectations of management was job security.

Similarly, the public schools adopted the industrial model to educate students to meet the needs of such a society. The respective roles of the teacher and the student were standardized, regardless of grade level or discipline. The teacher stood in front of the class, didactically presented the adopted curriculum, tested it, and graded student accomplishments. The students were sorted into classes and sat in rows and were expected to be obedient, to listen, to memorize, and to take tests that required them to reproduce "the" correct answers. If successful, the students were rewarded with passing grades. Ultimately, the schooling process culminated with a graduation ceremony that signified the students were ready to take their place as productive members of the industrial society.

As more and more students completed high school, however, society began to recognize the relationship and the benefits of a better educated individual and benefits of a better job. Parents began to prod their sons and daughters to continue their education in the hope that they would achieve a better life than the parents had experienced. This may have signalled the dawning of the information age. The number of students who sought to continue their education at the post-secondary level began to rise, regardless of their family background. In turn, the knowledge base of the individual and society as a whole began to increase.

In this respect, schools were outpacing the needs of the industrial society. Industry was still basically tied to the tried-and-true Taylor model. Access to information, the basis for knowledge, was still restricted to the management elite. Yet, more and more of the masses had access to knowledge through education. Slowly, an increasing number of people were making a living by using their brains, rather than their brawn. Technological advances in communications were making information and knowledge available to a greater segment of the population, not only in the U.S., but worldwide.

The final quantum leap that propelled the world into a global-information society was the "micro revolution." As individuals continued to require more information to do their jobs effectively, the microcomputer became a basic staple on the desks of service workers. These workers now had access to information, the raw material of knowledge, previously available only to the managerial elite. However, this new resource required workers to get to the essence of the information, to make sense of it, to make it meaningful and useful to the individual, to think and create new knowledge.

One immediate impact of this technological revolution was the redistribution of knowledge throughout the work force. It also became obvious that knowledge could not be mass produced. Knowledge not only became a valuable resource, but a necessity for survival in the information society. It is created in the minds of individuals, drawing on their experience, identifying the significant from the irrelevant, and making value judgments. An individual's worth could now be measured in terms of knowledge and skills that he or she possessed. No longer can the workers in an organization be viewed as the interchangeable commodities of the industrial age nor can they be discarded at will. Rather, workers must now be viewed as the new economic basis for the information society, replacing the agrarian society's possessions and the industrial society's money—a form of human capital.

*"The intellectual development of all students is the central purpose of school—for citizenship, economic well-being, and individual self-actualization."*

—A principal

## Human Capital, Security, and Schools

Change characterizes the information society. As we leave the industrial society, we are becoming a more diverse society. Unlike the successes of the industrial society, which mass produced goods for a mass society, success in the information society, when achieved, is temporary. If the U.S. is to build on its competitive strengths to build a better future, innovation is essential for survival. Meeting the diverse needs and wants in a pluralist population forces organizations to consider constant changes and improvements rather than stability.

nd complacency; risk rather than safety; ustomization rather than standardization; and, quality rather than quantity.

Furthermore, the use of old strategies to confront new problems will not vork. Albert Einstein said, "The world hat we have made as result of the level of hinking we have done hus far creates problems that we cannot olve at the same level s when they were created." When a problem arises that does not t into a readily identifiable frame of reference, our first instinct to ignore it and hope will go away. If the roblem persists, there is a tendency to etreat from the problem to "get back to asics" or to "get back on track."

Consider the plight of America's ndustrial giants. Employment by the Fortune 500 companies fell by more than 2 percent between 1977 and 1986, and he prediction is that they will trim at east 4 million more employees by the ear 2000. Staggering layoffs by GM, Sears, Boeing, and IBM tend to substantiate that prediction. Perhaps former GM Chairman Robert Stempel best ummed up America's situation when he tated, "We cannot blame our problems otally on the war, the plunge in consumer confidence, or the recession. Rather, we must make fundamental hanges in the way GM does business."

How will the U.S. deal with unemployment? During the 1980s, the U.S. kirted the real problem by creating new obs. However, the above figures indiate that this strategy will not work in today's age. Job security no longer comes from being employed, but rather from being employable. In the changing information society, employability implies a constant need for individuals to refine and upgrade their personal knowledge. In so doing, they will be increasing the nation's human capital.

> "*As we approach and go beyond the year 2000, our country and the world will need citizens with knowledge and skills developed for international understanding and the ability to use them as part of a team when solving problems which we cannot yet understand.*"
>
> —*A principal*

## The Answer Is the Question

Change is inevitable, but growth is optional. During the industrial era, the growth of schools in America coincided with the growth of industry. In fact, schools not only became indispensable institutions, but also large and loosely connected industrial conglomerates. Furthermore, much like the railroad people who thought they were in the railroad business, school people have come to believe that they are in the school business; teachers teach, administrators administer, supervisors supervise, etc. Many of the concerns within the school structure tend to focus more on adult working conditions than on student learning conditions. Have schools lost their focus on the students and learning? Can schools change to meet the needs of a changing society? Can schools produce learners who are prepared to enter the "real world" of today as productive members of society?

The very foundations of the industrial thinking have become firmly entrenched in the structure of American schools. Beliefs, such as "if it ain't broke, don't fix it," are signs of stagnation and a precursor to future problems. Yet, organizationally, schools have become huge bureaucratic conglomerates that are resistant to change or, at best, slow to react to change. How can we change the operations of the bureaucratic monolith we call schools, with the typical hierarchical structure that fosters power struggles and turf battles, top-down management, rules and regulations designed to ensure efficiency, laws enacted to address equity issues, unions that are more concerned with protecting their members than with their productivity, etc., to be more responsive to a changing society?

In an economy in which knowledge is becoming the premier wealth-producing resource, lifelong learning will not be a plus to an individual, but rather a necessity for all individuals. The industrial era model for schools was successful in preparing individuals to work in a factory or on an assembly line and in producing the information society of today. However, we need to consider the answers to a number of questions regarding the potential for our present schools to be successful in the future. Can we prepare students to enter a world of accelerating change and diversity, or continue to produce students with the one right answer to a question?

Can we create students who will question the truth of what they are taught, or blindly accept what they are taught as the truth? Can we create self-directed learners, or continue to create teacher-dependent role players? Can we integrate learning, or continue to teach a fragmented skills-based curriculum? Can we just afford to present students with the opportunity to learn, or must we devise means and methods to ensure that all students do learn? Can we devise performance-based student assessment schemes or continue to rely upon paper-and-pencil tests to determine a student's RAM? Can we find new and, or reallocate existing resources to educate all students, or face the loss of human capital? When confronting fierce international competition, only those organizations that can flexibly adapt to the notion that excellence is a state of becoming, rather than a state of being, stand a chance of survival.

To address the needs of society and student learning, the education community must constantly question, what is going on to foster learning? What is going on to deter learning and, what can we do to help? In essence, the answer to the question of where we have to go lies in our constant reflection on the questions.

> *"The directions and recommendations for change should be displayed on a continuum, i.e. improvement of schools is not a goal to be achieved, but a continuous, life-long process."*
> —A principal

> *"Improvements at the school level that last are those which are identified, understood, owned, and addressed by members of the school staff."*
> —A principal

# References

Benathy, B. "Designing Schools for a Global Village." *Educators Around the World Share Their Vision of a Design for School Year 2020.* Kansas City: Mid-Continent Regional Laboratory, 1990, pp. 35–37.

Coleman, J. S. *Policy Perspectives: Parental Involvement in Education.* Washington, D.C.: U.S. Department of Education, 1991.

Jacobson, S. L., and Conway, J. A. *Educational Leadership in an Age of Reform.* White Plains, N.Y.: Longman, 1990.

Kanter, R. M. *When Giants Learn To Dance.* New York: Simon & Schuster Inc., 1990.

McCarthy, M. J. *Mastering the Information Age.* Los Angeles: Jeremy P. Tarcher, Inc., 1991.

Naisbitt, J., and Aburdene, P. *Megatrends 2000: Ten New Directions for the 1990s.* New York: Avon Books, 1990.

———. *Megatrends: Ten New Directions Transforming Our Lives.* New York: Warner Books, 1982.

Pascale, R. T. *Managing on the Edge: How the Smartest Companies Use Conflict To Stay Ahead.* New York: Simon & Schuster, 1990.

Robinson, G. E. *Learning Expectancy: A Force Changing Education.* Arlington, Va.: Educational Research Service, 1986.

Rodriguez, R. *Hunger of Memory: The Education of Richard Rodriques.* Boston: Bantam Books, 1982.

Schlecty, P. C. *Schools for the Twenty-First Century.* San Francisco: Jossey-Bass, 1990.

Spady, W. G. "Organizing for Results: The Basis of Authentic Restructuring and Reform." *Educational Leadership* 46 (2): 4–8.

Toffler, A. *Power Shift.* New York: Bantam Books, 1990.

# CHAPTER 2

# Where Does School Reform Have To Go?

**B**efore continuing any journey, it is necessary to frequently assess where we are in relation to our destination. Just as the crew on a sailing vessel must constantly keep one eye on the horizon and one eye on the compass while making adjustments for changing wind and sea conditions, so too must the education community look to the future while assessing the present and make the necessary adaptations to ensure that we are on course. In education, we must be able to see beyond what is, to what could be.

## Reality and Dreams

When considering where we have to go, Peter Drucker has suggested that we should ask ourselves a number of crucial questions. The first set of questions involves purpose. What is the fundamental purpose of schools? What are their reasons for being? What is the business of schools?

The fundamental purpose of schools has not really changed since the inception of schools; it is to educate students. Even in an information society

> *"There must be a sense of urgency about the need to reconceptualize, without giving the impression that all schools are dysfunctional."*
>
> —*A principal*

where knowledge is constantly changing, we can reflect upon the notions of Jean Piaget to define our fundamental purpose. Educated people are individuals who are capable of doing new things, not simply repeating what other generations have done, individuals who are creative, who are inventive, and who can discover, individuals who are productive members of a democratic society. Such individuals need to use their minds to be critical and to verify, rather than just accept everything they are offered, and to recognize that learning is a lifelong process.

The second set of questions involves the future. While we cannot be sure of what the future will bring, we certainly should look at the current reality and trends that will allow us to ponder and project into the future. If we continue on our present course, what will our schools be like five years from now? Ten years from now? Will schools be able to fulfill their fundamental purpose in the future society? To answer these questions, we will need to look at the deep patterns of values, beliefs, and traditions formed over the course of the history of schools—the culture of schools. At the same time, we need to look at changes in the culture of the U.S. The first change affecting schools is in the demographics of this country, i.e., the aging of the population, the diversification of the family unit, and the transition from a nation with minorities to a nation of minorities. The second change influencing the kind of education that will be needed for the 21st century is the transition in the economic base of the U.S.

One of the concerns generated by the shift to an information/knowledge-based economy is the creation of a new caste system. It is an evolving system based on the access to information, and a resulting change in values. Information and knowledge are separating our society into an elite class and an underclass. If this becomes the case, we should also recognize that a society dichotomized by ignorance and knowledge will not share the same convictions, nor will it collectively perceive the same needs. Ignorance and knowledge rarely produce the same values. Therefore, unless schools can guarantee each individual equal access to information as a basis for knowledge such a dichotomized society may become a reality.

> "*We need to be even broader visionaries to fully include the range of social needs our clients bring to schools. Our staffs need to be educated to the fact that most of their formal training and nearly all their experiential knowledge is inappropriate and/or out of date for the students of the new century.*"
>
> —*A principal*

> "*I think it will take a lot of forward-looking people who do a great deal of thinking and research on their own, and who are student-oriented to establish the increased and futuristic kinds of expectations we will need to improve education.*"
>
> —*A principal*

The final critical question involves what must schools do today and tomorrow to be in the business we want to be in 10 years from now? The first thing we need to do to address this question is to recognize the abstract nature of the question. Rather than merely plotting a single trajectory from the reality of today to a point 10 years in the future, we need to think across the horizon of time and dream what it will be like when we arrive at our idyllic destination. We need to let our mind's eye see the possibilities inherent in the material we have stored there, not just look for the simple "quick-fix" concrete plan to begin our journey. In an abstract form, schools—past, present, and future—need to develop organizations that reflect and are compatible with their cultural environments.

The culture of a society is a historically rooted, socially transmitted set of deep patterns of thinking and ways of acting that give meaning to human experience. These patterns unconsciously dictate how experience is seen, assessed, and acted on. The culture of our schools describes the character of school as it reflects the values, beliefs, and traditions that formed over a period of time. Essentially, schools are microcosms of the expectations a society has for its children. They are the institutions by which society creates the conditions for its perpetuation.

## From Dreams to Reality, From Purpose to Goals

Since schools provide the experiences for cultural and knowledge transmission, they will need to change their focus of maintaining the existing state and operating in an autonomous closed-system mode which is separate from other societal agencies. Rather, schools will need to become integrated with all the other societal systems in a cooperative and coordinated relationship. They will need to reflect and interpret the society as well as shape the society through interactions, as a future creating, innovative, and open societal system that embraces all the domains of human and societal existence.

In an information society, knowledge fuels the economy and shapes society. This is accomplished by way of the product of our schools—the educated individual. Therefore, all students in our schools need to be taught how to define what information they need, know how to find it, and how to use it. They will need to be able to envision the interconnectedness of everything. All students will need to be guaranteed access to the same educational opportunities and the same knowledge and, through them, to upward mobility, whatever their

> *"The attitude that all students can learn must be shared by everyone in our schools."*
> —A principal

> *"We need to look at the real world issues far more than we do and bring these issues to all our students in a context that will help them develop the self-confidence to deal with real issues and a strong work ethic."*
> —A principal

origin, wealth, or previous schooling.

Can this dream become a vision of reality in our schools? Can *all* students learn? Reflect on the work of Ron Edmonds and ask, how many effective schools would I have to see to be persuaded of the educability of all students? The key to making this vision become a reality resides in the reaffirmation of the fundamental purpose of schools and the creation of a vision of schools that is consistent with this purpose. Regardless of the manner in which the purpose is stated, it must be based on the internalized belief of everyone connected with schools that all students can learn and that all students will learn if they are presented with the right opportunities. If this belief is accepted, then school personnel can envision that the students in the school of the future will produce knowledge, not simply receive it. In turn, they will also be able to picture students capable of growing up to be vital, significant, self-aware, and reflective adults capable of living useful lives in a democratic information society. Thus, the dream can become a vision that can be transformed into reality.

As schools attempt to implement their vision for the future, they will need to begin and/or continue to work on a number of fronts consistent with their fundamental purpose. This purpose refers to the schools' reason for being. It does not refer to goals. Yet the two are connected. Goals are set and pursued so that the purpose may be fulfilled. Goals are targets, while the purpose has to do with values and commitments.

The realization of the importance of education to the welfare of the U.S. society was under-scored when the governors and President Bush announced six national goals for public education in February 1989. In setting forth these goals and the agenda for education in the 1990s and beyond, it will be important to keep the goals in perspective so that we do not lose sight of our purpose and allow the goals to become ends in themselves. What has not been stated regarding these goals is that while they have been set forth for public education, they are inextricably interwoven in all facets and segments of our society. As a result, many people have questioned whether the achievement of these goals is realistic or "pie-in-the-sky" political rhetoric?

Regardless of one's position on the goals, they have focused our attention on many of the problems and needs of the information society. Furthermore, as we have begun to look in earnest at the goals, it has become evident that the complexities of the problems will not be solved by our schools in isolation from U.S. society as a whole. While there will certainly be no simple solutions to these problems, perhaps we should be asking ourselves a more important question—can we afford not to achieve them? If we accept these challenges, they will test our ingenuity, resourcefulness, determination, and char-

acter. But, they will also provide us with numerous opportunities to move closer to our vision of a better educated, and hence a more productive, society.

> *"Maybe the established national educational goals are not entirely attainable, but I do believe they are approachable, even though there is a lot more to them than meets the eye."*
>
> —*A principal*

## Goals and Problems, Problems and Goals

As we look more closely at each of the six goals, it will be easy to identify a number of the major problems our schools will face in attempting to achieve them. Identifying the causes of each problem will not be easy. Nonetheless, we will need to be problem finders before attempting to be problem solvers. As such, the questions we pose may prove to be more important than our answers, since simplistic answers to complex problems will probably not lead us to where we want and need to go. This is not to say that schools have not been striving to achieve their fundamental purpose and achieving some success, but rather that we must continue to seek to achieve success for all students.

## Goal #1 — *By the year 2000, all children in America will start school ready to learn.*

At first glance, who could argue with this goal? Upon closer inspection, however, a number of questions arise for schools. First, readiness for learning is generally associated with the average age of a group of children who are considered to be at a particular level of the developmental process when they have the capacity to undertake the learning of specific material. On the other hand, readiness for school tends to focus more specifically on cognitive, affective, and psychomotor skill development, i.e., linguistic skills, printing and drawing, school adaptation skills, social skills, fine and gross motor skills, etc. Should children who are not developmentally ready be kept out of school, or can the development of children be stimulated by the learning activities that occur in schools?

While this question is being debated, we should also consider what we know about preschool children. It is estimated that at least 33 percent of U.S. children are at risk of school failure even before they enter kindergarten; that 6.7 percent are born each year with lower than normal birth weights, thereby increasing the likelihood they will require special education services; that 20 percent of all handicapped children would not be handicapped if the mother had received just one physical examination in the first trimester of pregnancy; and, that 25 percent of all preschool children in the U.S. have lived in poverty, the highest rate of any industrialized nation. Rather than considering how ready children are to start school, perhaps we should question how ready parents are to become parents? While we have little control with regard to parenting, the fate of children before they enter schools is really in the hands of the family, church, health-care providers, and social service institutions.

> "*Schools are now required to provide services that the community, families, churches, and other agencies do or should provide to some students. What we need is more parent involvement in the total development and education of their children from day one.*"
>
> —*A principal*

Second, how will readiness to learn be assessed? When pondering this question, one should consider that there is considerable debate among scholars given the rapid, sporadic, and highly individualized nature of growth in young children. Yet, when focusing on the readiness needs of *all* students, it is interesting to reflect on how well we are addressing the needs of those children who have been identified as being in need. Today, only 40 percent of children eligible for Head Start services receive them.

Third, what types of intervention are appropriate? Since young children vary on virtually every measurable characteristic, matching instructional strategies and learning modalities will be critical in accommodating individual needs. Equally important is the necessity that appropriate services be made available to all children on an equitable basis.

Certainly, we have a long way to go to achieve this goal. However, it should also be clear that the responsibility for achieving this goal does not rest solely upon the schools, but rather that parents must be meaningfully involved in the solution to these problems. The question we will need to address is whether or not schools and various public and private sector providers of early childhood care and education can work collaboratively and cooperatively with parents to achieve this goal?

## Goal #2 — By the year 2000, the high school graduation rate will increase to at least 90 percent.

The considerable amount of attention that has been paid to this goal by the media, society, and schools may be one indication that we are beginning to recognize the importance of education to the information society. It may also be due to the fact that dropouts can be reported in a single numerical figure that is easily understood by the general public. At any rate, dropout data have also been used as one of the prime weapons to indicate that schools are "not doing their jobs."

What is not reported is the fact that from 1910 to 1965, the percent of students who graduated from high school continued to rise from 10 percent to approximately 75 percent, depending upon how you define a dropout. It should be noted that these figures were achieved during a period of time when the primary concern of society was to provide all students with an opportunity to learn and prior to efforts to address equity issues for minorities and special needs students. Furthermore, by 1989, 87 percent of Americans between the ages of 25 and 29 held high school diplomas or GED certificates, and 91 percent of the class of 1980 had completed high school or its equivalent by 1986.

Nonetheless, a number of questions need to be asked with regard to this goal.

> "*We all want students to succeed. Maybe that's why we subconsciously tend to work with the better students—those who we feel have the best chance to succeed. Since many of these students will make it with or without our help, maybe we should concentrate more of our time on those students who are most in need, especially those in urban settings.*"
>
> —*A principal*

The first is how do we define a dropout? If we consider a dropout as a person who is not in school and has not graduated from high school, the dropout rate for the U.S. in 1986 was reported as 11.9 percent. But the problems associated with dropout rates and the individuals who drop out of school go much deeper than a single figure.

The second question is what is the impact of dropouts on society? Economically, dropouts earn on average 20 percent less than high school graduates. Each year's class of dropouts costs $250 billion over their lifetimes in lost wages and in foregone taxes. From a social perspective, dropouts have higher unemployment rates since they lack the knowledge and skills of graduates. In turn, this increases the need for and cost of social services and increased crime, and reduces political participation in our society. Psychologically, higher unemployment is associated with higher mortality rates, higher suicide rates, and higher rates of admission to mental hospitals. Therefore, students who drop out of school create a larger drain on society's resources than if they remained in school, and for a much longer period of time.

Finally, we need to recognize what we know about dropouts. It is estimated that more than 10 million children between the ages of 3 and 17 suffer from developmental, learning, or emotional problems that could interfere with their progress in school. Many of these stu-

*16*

lents may be at risk of dropping out of chool for a number of environmental reasons that could be addressed. The maior concerns, poverty and cultural differences, although not the whole story, play a major role in determining who drops out. Some of these characteristics can be traced to the students' family, i.e., low-income families, single-parent homes, home alone three or more hours per day, and parents with a low level of education and limited English proficiency.

Other students become at risk because of problems that develop in adolescence, i.e., held back one or more grades in school, teen pregnancy, criminal conviction, suicide attempts, and alcohol and/or drug abuse. Since most of these characteristics are found in much higher concentrations among minorities and in urban settings, there can be little wonder why the inner-city schools, where the dropout figure is as high as 50 percent, face such special problems.

Ironically, if you equalize the environment in which a minority person lives, you will tend to equalize his or her educational achievement as well. For people of similar social and economic background, race tends to fade as a predictor of educational achievement. Based upon these research findings, we need to consider whether or not we can afford to lose any percentage of our future workers, whether or not we are willing to accept the challenge of working with at-risk students, and whether or not we are willing to take the responsibility for re-

> "*To focus on intellectual development will require the reconceptualization of what counts as learning*—from *delivering educational services to passive student receivers*, to *active learning and construction of meaning by students in all disciplines, i.e., learning how to learn?*"
>
> —*A principal*

covering individuals once they have dropped out of school.

**Goal #3 — *By the year 2000, American students will leave grades 4, 8, and 12 having demonstrated competency in challenging subject matter, including English, mathematics, science, history, and geography; and every school in America will ensure that all students learn to use their minds well, so that they may be prepared for responsible citizenship, further learning, and productive employment in our modern economy.***

This goal speaks directly to the fundamental purpose of schools and the product of the teaching-learning process in terms of student outcomes. It also addresses some of the major concerns and recommendations outlined in the *SCANS Report, Workforce 2000,* and *America's Choice: High Skills or Low Wages,* which outline the need for a highly skilled and productive work force in an information society.

Before responding to this goal, it might be prudent to assess the effectiveness of our current efforts in this regard. As we complete our transition from an industrial society to an information society, good jobs will require increasing levels of skill and knowledge. Unless schools can address this need for all students, there is an increasing probability of a "skills gap" or "mismatch" in which high-skilled jobs go unfilled while low-skilled people are in excess supply. As a result, U.S. competitiveness in a global economy and equality will both suffer.

Over the past two decades, U.S. productivity growth has slowed to a crawl. From 1960 to 1973, American private, nonagricultural workers each produced an average of 2.9 percent more every year than the year before. Since 1973, productivity growth has fallen to approximately 1 percent per year. Because the economic growth that the U.S. experienced in the 1980s was a result of the increase in the number of people working in our society, from 40 percent to 50 percent, rather than an increase in worker productivity, our wages have not improved. In fact, real average weekly earnings have dropped more than 12 percent since 1969. These hardships, however, have not been borne equally by all Americans.

Since 1967, the highest earning 30 percent of American families increased their share of the national income from 54 percent to 58 percent in 1987, while the bottom 70 percent of American families have been losing ground. Furthermore, while the earnings of college-educated males age 24 to 34 increased by 10 percent, the earnings of those with only high school diplomas declined by 9 percent. To put these figures in a future context, consider that it has been estimated that four-year college graduates have been increasing as a percentage of our work force since 1940, when 6 percent were college graduates, to a projected 30 percent in the year 2000. Since it has been estimated that more than 70 percent of U.S. jobs will not require a college education by the year 2000, we appear to be on target for meeting this particular need.

While these observations are interesting, consideration should be given to projections that our population is growing at a slower rate than for any period since the 1950s. By the year 2000, more than 40 percent of the new work force entrants will be minorities and immigrants, groups which are at disproportionately low income levels today. Yet, it will be these workers who will serve as the backbone of our economy, and their productivity on the job will make or break our economic future. The potential consequences for our entire society, if our productivity continues to falter, if our real wages continue to stagnate or decline, and if our wage gap continues to widen between the educational "haves" and "have nots," could be a slide into relative poverty—for all members of our society.

How does this relate to the fundamental purpose of schools? SCANS has identified five competencies and a three-part foundation of skills and personal qualities needed for solid job performance. If our front-line workers are to compete in the economic arena, they will need to compete in the educational arena. However, most of our schools are oriented toward the needs of the college bound student. On the other hand, schools tend to expect and to produce minimal educational effort or achievement among students who are not college bound. The tragedy of the "teach the best and forget the rest" philosophy is that we communicate to millions of students every year, especially low income and minority students, that we do not believe they have what it takes to learn. When these students live down to our expectations, despite evidence that they can think and meet very high performance standards under the right conlitions, we can always cite their lack of progress as evidence for our actions.

Are we prepared to redistribute the limited resources of schools to ensure that all students have an opportunity to meet this national goal? Bud Hodgkinson has noted that, at present, we concentrate our resources on those least likely to fail, while the "bottom third" of our young people are more likely to fail than the "bottom third" of any nation with which we usually compare ourselves. Our "non-college" students tend to be relegated to "general curriculum" courses to learn "life survival skills," which results in their exposure to less-qualified teachers, less time devoted to instruction, less extensive and less challenging content, and a less positive classroom learning environment.

Finally, we need to be concerned about how students will be assessed when they leave grades 4, 8, and 12? Will there be standards and, if so, who will set the standards? Again, we must concern ourselves with America's fascination with simplistic testing results that are supposed to measure the complexities of student learning. Such testing is primarily controlled by commercial publishers who produce norm-referenced, multiple-choice instruments designed to rank students cheaply and efficiently, not to enhance instruction nor to assist in making informed curricular decisions. There are a number of areas in a school's curriculum which do not easily lend themselves to norm-referenced assessment. We will need to devise alternative means of assessments that will allow student performances and exhibitions, along with oral and written examinations, to demonstrate their learning proficiencies.

If our schools are to meet the challenges of the information society, they will need to determine what they are doing well and what changes need to be made to improve student learning. To this end, we will need to question how schools can gain public support for the changes they feel are necessary to improve student learning.

> *"If we're not already number one in math and science, it would seem to me that we are very close. But not for all students."*
>
> —A principal

## Goal #4 — By the year 2000, U.S. students will be first in the world in mathematics and science achievement.

Of all the national goals, this particular goal may be the most troubling. It would seem to imply that U.S. students are currently behind the students of other countries in international comparisons of science and mathematics achievement. It has been reported that the U.S. ranks somewhere between the middle and last place in international comparisons of science and mathematics achievement. However, a number of scholars have speculated that these relative rankings are biased by a number of important methodological problems. These concerns range from the percentages of students in the various nations for the way in which the results were reported, to whether or not the reported student results represented all students in that nation.

In spite of these concerns, there are a number of indicators that would lead one to conclude that the U.S. is already number one in the world of science, mathematics, and technology. It has been estimated that there are more than 40,000 professional journals in the areas of science and mathematics with scientists, mathematicians, and researchers writing articles for those journals at a rate in excess of one million per year. In those journals of engineering, mathematics, biomedical research, physics, earth and space sciences, chemistry, and biology, Americans accounted for 30-40 percent of all the published articles. Great Britain, Japan, and the former Soviet Union were all tied for second place with about 8 percent of the articles. Furthermore, foreign student enrollment in the sciences at U.S. universities continues to be high. Indeed, it is generally acknowledged that our system of higher education offers a greater variety and quality of research opportunities than any other nation.

While we could argue that our secondary schools have given rise to the scientists, mathematicians, and researchers in our colleges and universities, few of us would contend that all students receive the same quality of science and mathematics instruction within the same school. Schools have long assumed that only students with special talents, usually males, can become proficient in science and mathematics. These students tend to be a relatively small percentage of those students who will go on to college. For the remainder of students, traditional teaching in science is restricted to courses that emphasize large amounts of superficial information to be memorized and in mathematics courses that bear no clear relationship to scientific research or problem solving. In these predominant methods of teaching science and mathematics, students spend years learning facts and skills before it is assumed they can

begin to think or use science and mathematics productively.

Unfortunately, science and mathematics are thought to be different and virtually insulated from the other disciplines in school, accessible to only a select few, and, except for basic computation, of little relevance or use for most people. Viewed from this perspective, what is often taught to students is fundamentally rote memorization, devoid of real meaning. Such teaching focuses on detailed facts and procedures while neglecting the fundamental nature and value of the field. To be meaningful, we will need to redesign instruction in these disciplines to give greater emphasis to major scientific concepts, scientific issues in the context of public policy, research methodology, statistics, and problem solving for all students. Furthermore, we will need to integrate these disciplines with other curriculum areas for all students and relate science and mathematics learning to beneficial results in terms of the welfare and productivity of our society as a whole.

**Goal #5 — By the year 2000, every adult American will be literate and will possess the skills necessary to compete in a global economy and to exercise the rights and responsibilities of citizenship.**

The prognosis for achieving the adult literacy portion of this goal in our lifetime is optimistically grim. To consider such an achievement within 10 year is virtually impossible. Our current efforts in this regard rely heavily on volunteer learners and volunteer, part-time teachers. As a result of the existing adult literacy programs, which cost approxinately $200 million in federal and state funds, only about 3 percent of the adults who are in need of such services receive them. However, if we redirect our focus to the five specific subgoals specified by the governors and the President, it certainly seems plausible that we can improve upon our current situation.

To meet this goal, we will need to rethink our current schemes and our allocation of resources. Schools, with the aid and assistance of business, develop new industry-specific professional and technical training programs for occupations that do not require a four-year baccalaureate degree. Working jointly, schools must look to assist employers and employees seeking to become high performance work organizations and workers. Similarly, government and community-based organizations must be willing, with the assistance of schools, to reorganize existing programs to create new comprehensive, coherent employment and training systems that are driven by the needs of clients. Finally, schools, in conjunction with the public and private sectors of society, will need to be willing to promote and support those qualified students, especially minorities, to enter post-secondary institutions of higher education.

The second portion of this goal deals with an aspect of life that is currently the subject of intense scrutiny and discussion in American life and which is stated in Goal #3—citizenship. The duties and responsibilities of good citizenship transcend the cognitive and psychomotor thinking processes, skills, and abilities that individuals must possess to be productive members of society. The characteristics of good citizenship embody the beliefs and values society desires in individuals, as well as the outcomes of the educational process.

> "*If adults demonstrate the importance of learning as a lifelong process, then maybe the attitudes of students toward school would be different.*"
>
> —*A principal*

Being a good citizen requires good role models. Being a good role model in a democratic society requires that an individual be aware of and seeks to understand civic issues from various perspectives, actively participate in the deliberations involving these issues, and participate in the election of the individuals who will establish the policies governing the issues. Furthermore, the duties and responsibilities of good citizenship include abiding by the laws of society, concern for the welfare of others, respect for other members of the community, integrity in one's actions, honesty, fairness, fidelity, and personal accountability in the pursuit of excellence. In essence, serving as a role model for good citizenship requires that individuals develop and live by high ethical standards in both their personal and public lives.

Unfortunately, a number of high profile individuals in both the private and public sectors have failed to meet these high standards. As a result, many individuals have become disenfranchised from the feeling of being a member of a community and the governance of our democratic society. If we are to flourish as a society, then instilling the duties and responsibilities of good citizenship in each and every student and adult in our society is as paramount to becoming an educated individual as the thought processes and skills which we generally consider to be functions of the education. Melding the high ideals and values of our democratic society while assisting others in pursuing the cognitive and psychomotor skills for all students and adults is certainly a comprehensive means to educating the whole individual.

Since the achievement of all aspects of this goal will require the left hand to know what the right hand is doing, we will need to open a meaningful dialog between schools, businesses, government, and associated organizations. The questions we need to ask are, will these organizations and agencies be willing to actively participate in a consortium to address this goal? And, will they be able to look in the mirror and honestly say that they are serving as a role model for good citizenship?

*" We may be able to get most of the drugs and violence out of most schools, but it will still exist in the larger society. Then what?"*

—*A principal*

## Goal #6 — By the year 2000, every school in America will be free of drugs and violence and will offer a disciplined environment conducive to learning.

The achievement of this goal has been at or near the top of the agenda for schools for nearly 20 years. However, as with the other goals, the issues involved in drug-free schools and in a disciplined environment will not be achieved solely by schools.

First, the reports on the use of drugs by school-aged youth vary. One report has indicated that the typical high school of 1,000 students has 437 students who will smoke pot, 103 who will try cocaine, 83 who will try LSD, and 13 who will use heroin. However, most of the abuse does not take place primarily in schools as some adults in society might think. In fact, many schools are substantially drug free today. Yet, the same cannot be said for other public places, i.e., parks, malls, concert halls, sports arenas, etc., nor can it be said for many homes. This does not mean that drug use by students is not a problem for schools nor that some drug use does not occur in our schools. What this does point to is need for assistance that goes beyond the educational programs of our schools.

Second, the adolescent drug problem is a relatively recent phenomenon in terms of our society and our schools. Prior to the mid 1960s, drug use by school-age children was almost nonexistent. One decade later, it was an epidemic. Since this was a new problem to many adults in society, they found themselves unprepared to deal with it. In many cases, parents put on blinders and refused to admit that their sons and daughters were involved with illicit drug use.

Other parents, although not condoning drug use, drew a line between addiction and the casual or "recreational" use of drugs, especially those with which they were familiar, such as alcohol. Still other parents sought to blame or punish adolescent drug users. However, few adults took time to reflect upon the messages that adults projected to adolescents. What are children to think when they hear their adult role models tell them to "just say no" to drugs, but see laws violated by these very same people, or laws that are not enforced?

Third, regardless where parents stood on the issue of drug abuse, there can be little doubt that they considered this problem to be serious. Unfortunately, their preoccupation with the drug issues, with the economic and social issues involved in being a parent, and with their own work, other aspects of a student's social and academic behavior in schools paled by comparison. Why were schools making such a big deal about violations of school rules and regulations, minor disruptions to the classroom environments, failure to complete assignments, failure to attend school, etc., when there were such larger issues to be dealt with? Similarly, some school personnel questioned the same things. The result has been an increasing breakdown in home-school relations, in spite of the effective schools research that points to this as a factor which fosters learning in schools.

While there is no simple answer to achieving this goal, it would appear that the solution will again require a collaborative and cooperative effort between our schools, governmental agencies, private and public organizations and agencies, and parents. A clear consensus, firm policy, and decisive action will be needed to move the nation toward the goal of drug-free schools. This action will need to confront the supply, the distribution, and the use of drugs. To this end, there is recent evidence that there has been a decline in certain forms of youthful drug use, but the war on drugs has not been won. The question may ultimately be, do we as a society have the resolve to deal with the problem of drugs and discipline within our schools?

## Purpose, Dreams, and Common Themes

In an attempt to focus our dreams into a clear vision for the future, we will undoubtedly encounter a variety of social, economic, and political pressures and values that will seem to make the vision difficult to achieve. Nonetheless, if we continue to strive to make our vision a reality, we may uncover a number of common themes that will aid us in fulfilling our fundamental purpose. As we develop a vision of education for the next century, as we address our national goals, as we conclude the transition to an information society, three common themes are of central importance.

> *"Schools are value-driven institutions. Those values that generate student and teacher successes need to be identified and promulgated."*
> —*A principal*

First, schools must provide success for all students and teachers. We must not just pay lip service to the statement that all students can learn, we need to affirm and internalize this belief by ensuring that all students do learn and do achieve success in school. We will need to look closely at our present stratification practices that preclude certain students from access to higher levels of achievement in particular disciplines. Furthermore, we should make every effort to see that no student is labeled as likely to fail because of the social, economic, or racial characteristics of their families or of their communities.

Second, we must serve the whole child. We will need to recognize that the social, emotional, physical, and academic growth and development of the individual child are inextricably linked. Therefore, if we are to foster the cognitive and the academic development of students in our schools, all other facets of development must be addressed. To avoid duplication of efforts and to attain maximum effectiveness, efforts by schools, by families, and by the other institutions that affect the individual student will need to be coordinated. In turn, this will require that each of these social institutions maintain an open and collaborative dialog relative to their individual missions, goals, etc.

> "*It would take a great deal of cooperation between schools, home, and the community.*"
>
> —*A principal*

Finally, we must develop a shared responsibility for the total development of the individual student. Since the responsibilities of the school, the family, and other community organizations and agencies are shared and overlapping in many cases, we will need to reflect upon their purposes and practices to meet the needs of individual children. Furthermore, these key institutions will need to reexamine their respective rules, roles, relationships, and responsibilities as they relate to one another in order to promote the social and academic development of all children.

# References

Bracey, G. W. "Why Can't They Be Like We Were?" *Phi Delta Kappan* 73 (2): 104–17.

Chubb, T. E., and Moe, T. M. *Politics, Markets, and America's Schools.* Washington, D.C.: The Brookings Institution, 1990.

Colton, D. L. "Vision." *National Forum* 65 (2): 33–35.

Darling-Hammond, L. "Achieving Our Goals: Superficial or Structural Reforms?" *Phi Delta Kappan* 72 (4): 286–95.

Davies, D. "Schools Reaching Out: Family, School and Community Partnerships for Student Success." *Phi Delta Kappan* 72 (5): 376–82.

Deal, T. E., and Peterson, K. D. *The Principal's Role in Shaping School Culture.* Washington, D.C.: U.S. Department of Education, 1990.

Drucker, P. F. *The New Realities.* New York: Harper & Row, 1990.

Duttweiler, P. C., and Mutchler, S. E. *Organizing the Educational System for Excellence: Harnessing the Energy of People.* Austin, Tex.: Southwest Educational Development Laboratory, 1990.

Gage, N. L. "Dealing with the Dropout Problem." *Phi Delta Kappan* 72 (4): 280–85.

Hawley, R. A. "The Bumpy Road to Drug-Free Schools." *Phi Delta Kappan* 72 (4): 310–14.

Hodgkinson, H. L. *Beyond the Schools.* Arlington, Va.: American Association of School Administrators and National School Boards Association, 1991.

——. "Reform Versus Reality." *Phi Delta Kappan* 73 (1): 9–16.

Kagan, S. L. "Readiness 2000: Rethinking Rhetoric and Responsibility." *Phi Delta Kappan* 72 (4): 272–79.

Kouzes, J. M., and Posner, B. Z. *The Leadership Challenge.* San Francisco: Jossey-Bass, 1987.

McCarthy, M. J. *Mastering the Information Age.* Los Angeles: Jeremy F. Tarcher, Inc., 1991.

Mikulecky, L. "National Adult Literacy and Lifelong Learning Goals." *Phi Delta Kappan* 72 (4): 304–09.

National Center on Education and the Economy. *America's Choice: High Skills or Low Wages!* Rochester, N.Y.: National Center on Education and the Economy, 1990.

National Commission on Children. *Beyond Rhetoric: A New American Agenda for Children and Families.* Washington, D.C.: Author, 1991.

Rotberg, I. C. "I Never Promised You First Place." *Phi Delta Kappan* 72 (4): 296–303.

Schlecty, P. C. *Schools for the Twenty-First Century.* San Francisco: Jossey-Bass, 1990.

Secretary's Commission on Achieving Necessary Skills. *What Work Requires of Schools: A SCANS Report for America 2000.* Washington, D.C.: U.S. Department of Labor, 1991.

Sizer, T. R. *Horace's Compromise: The Dilemma of the American High School.* Boston: Houghton-Mifflin, 1984.

White, M. A. "Education in the Information Age." *Educators Around the World Share Their Vision of a Design for School Year 2020.* Kansas City: Mid-Continent Regional Laboratory (1990): 11–13.

# CHAPTER 3

# What Does School Reform Mean to People?

Our system of public education in the U.S. has been the primary agent for the tremendous advances in our nation during the past century. Some will profess that we have accepted and implemented the Jeffersonian ideal, to educate every individual to his or her fullest potential, through our public schools. After all, haven't the products of our current educational system, the educated individuals, been responsible for the great number of advances over the years in medicine, science, and technology? Aren't we seeing these advances occur at an accelerating pace? Haven't we witnessed tremendous changes throughout the world and the beginning of a new world order? Since the answer is obviously yes, then the question becomes, why change a system that is working?

Perhaps it is because of our past successes that we must look at our present system of education and determine if this system will get us to where we want to go. Since we can enumerate countless success stories, why is there such heated debates over educational reform? Why, if we proudly hold our education system up to the rest of the world as the model for educating all students, rather than just the best, do we demean its outcomes at home? Do we need to radically reform the system, or merely make some course corrections? Should we enshrine the system, or entomb it? While many people believe that we have and are implementing our fundamental purpose, beliefs, and ideals for schools, there are also many people who believe that "it just ain't necessarily so."

Regardless of one's perspective on these issues, educators are quick to note the numerous reform efforts or school improvement processes that are currently underway in our schools. This points to one of two conclusions—the system is in need of change, or the system is already constantly changing to meet changing needs. In either case, however, these efforts focus on improving the system we already have rather than imagining a totally different system. Furthermore, many of these efforts tend to come in the form

> "*Restructuring will require a commitment from all involved to establish an attitude that the development of new and creative institutions for teaching and learning are essential for the future of this country.*"
>
> —*A principal*

of top-down mandates, which rarely achieve their anticipated results; to concentrate on how to do things right, rather than if we are doing the right things; to be directed toward things, rather than people; and, to be based upon old paradigms, rather than searching for new paradigms. As a result, the system retains its traditional structure with schools changing, but still unchanged. Charles Mojowski has summarized most of the present reform efforts by observing that the individuals responsible for these efforts "continue to believe that, with just a few more horses and a few more men, they too can put Humpty-Dumpty back together again."

> *"I'm not sure that simply doing more of what we're already not doing well is any answer. More isn't always better. Sometimes it's more of the wrong stuff."*
>
> —*A principal*

> *"The academic progress of students will only begin to improve when what goes on in the classroom and in the schools changes, regardless of the directives of the system or the structure of the system."*
>
> —*A principal*

## Tinkering or Systemwide Change

Whether citing the successes or failures of education, we tend to speak in such inanimate terms as the school and the system. But, education is not an object that can be tuned up, fixed, or tinkered with in a piecemeal, fragmented, or incremental fashion at periodic intervals. Education is not about things; it is about people. This social system is about unlocking the potential and the creativity that lies within each and every student, teacher, and administrator. It is about building on our successes and learning from our failures, and it is about the changes and growth of people over a period of time. Education is a holistic living process made up of interacting and interdependent systems. As such, changes in one system or one part of a system require adjustments by all parts of the educational process.

To begin the process of systemwide restructuring, individuals at all levels in the existing organization will need to look at the *rules* of the district. The rules are generally organized as the formal and informal policies adopted from the school district level down to the classroom level and the district contractual agreements. In essence, the policies and agreements represent the common understandings about what is and what ought to be. They are established to denote the behaviors that are critical to a district's, a school's, or a classroom's functioning and embody the values and beliefs of that level in the organization.

The adoption of formal rules may be a symbolic sign of the degree of authority, control, and power that individuals or groups possess at the various levels within the organization. On the other hand, the informal rules actually represent the way things get done. Assessing the degree to which the formal and informal rules are congruent may provide valuable information regarding the sharing of values and beliefs among all members of the social system.

Ideally, rules are established to promote and ensure equity and excellence in the delivery of services. From a practical perspective, however, these ideals co-exist in a dynamic tension since the equal treatment of unequals is inherently unequal. Therefore, educational reform will need to review and reassess whether or not the formal and informal rules reflect a common vision of what "ought to be," rather than the pragmatic day-to-day reality of "what is."

Second, a school system will need to review the *roles* that have been established for individuals within the organization. These roles, again both formal and informal, define the way an individual acts and functions within the system. Implicit in the roles are the expectations for all persons occupying a given position in the social order as they deal with other people.

Typically, the individual roles within a school system are defined in a hierarchical and stereotypical manner on an organizational chart. Each role has specific duties and responsibilities with implicit, if not explicit, limits on the authority of the individual. Initially and ideally, attempts are made to fill specific roles with people who possess the characteristics, skills, and knowledge to meet the expectations of the role. In most instances, the selection or assignment of an individual to a role must comply with specific personnel rules, although contractual agreements as well as discrimination, nepotism, patronage, and longevity of the "good-old boy" system

are often political factors in such decisions. However, once the role is filled, rarely is consideration given to the changing needs within the social system, nor the changing characteristics, skills, or knowledge that the individual must possess to be effective in that role.

If the public educational system is to reform, consideration will need to be given to matching the expertise of individuals with the task at hand, rather than assigning the task to a position. This will require the rules of the system to be both flexible and adaptable to meet changing needs. To achieve this end, we will need to consider breaking the stereotypical role divisions, to flattening the organizational structure, and to increasing the professional decision-making ability of all the personnel in the organization.

While this may sound reasonable or even desirable, we should recognize that there will be a number of personal and interpersonal barriers to changes in organizational roles and they may be formidable. Many individuals will be satisfied with the status quo. Some may be reluctant to assume new responsibilities, and others may fear losing power or taking risks. In any case, the reorganization of roles within a school district will be threatening to many individuals and will need to be approached with extreme caution.

A third factor in a systemwide restructuring of a school system deals with interpersonal *relationships*. In terms of an

> *"It is important to realize that flexibility, not rigid rules, are going to be needed for schools to make the changes needed."*
>
> —A principal

> *"Schools need to emphasize the team concept. We need to stop worrying about if something is my job, or your job—it's our job."*
>
> —A principal

organization, a social relationship exists when, as a result of a common focus, one person's behavior elicits a dependable and expected response from another person. The extent to which similar responses tend to follow particular requests is an indication of the effectiveness of the relationship.

If we are to work cooperatively and collaboratively, we will need to promote positive relationships between all human resources within the school system and the community. To this end, perhaps the keys to effective relationships are the mutual trust and respect that individuals or groups of individuals possess for one another. In this regard, those factors are not necessarily bequeathed by one's position in the formal structure of a school system. Rather, the degree of trust and respect between two people is something that is earned over a period of time.

Within a school system, positive working relations can be achieved if individuals can accept and understand the dynamics of relationships in various situations. All positive relationships, formal or informal, share a number of characteristics. The primary prerequisites of positive relationships are that they have a common vision and that they exist in a positive social culture and climate.

Once these characteristics have been established, relationships tend to be horizontal rather than vertical. They are flexible and are able to reconfigure themselves quickly to meet changing needs and/or conditions. Leadership in them tends to be based on competence and personality, rather than on social or organizational rank. Power turns over frequently and more easily than in a typical bureaucracy, changing hands as new situations demand new expertise.

The relationships between and among administrators, teachers, students, parents, community members, and external agencies may all be subject to restructuring efforts depending upon the situation. Nonetheless, changes in existing relationships may need to be approached cautiously for many of the same reasons noted previously for changing roles. However, if we can portray all the individuals and groups who may interact with the school system as learners, we will be ready for cooperative learning relationships. Finally, if we position these individuals and groups in a collegial relationship from the start, we will be more likely to emphasize our commonalities than our differences.

> "*There will have to be trust, and a common mission among school personnel for them to really work.*"
> —*A principal*

A fourth factor to consider in school reform is *responsibility*. A look at the meaning of the word responsibility—the ability to choose a response—to answer for one's actions or decisions, may be at the crux of the problem in many school systems. We are all responsible for our own personal actions in our personal lives because we can exercise the authority to make decisions regarding our actions. Within a school system, however, administrators, teachers, and students are frequently given duties and responsibilities but no authority to act outside the prescribed rules. Yet, many of the situations, problems, and opportunities that we come in contact with do not fit neatly within the existing rules.

If we truly want all the people employed by a school system to assume responsibility and be accountable for their actions, then we will need to treat them accordingly. We will need to look not only at decisions but the decision-making process within schools and school systems as well. At present, most systems are built upon rules and hierarchical structures that treat people as technicians. Tasks are generally designated for specific roles within the system or delegated to individuals who are expected to faithfully follow detailed policies prepared by others. Those individuals are then monitored by people in positions of higher status in the system who often do not know the specific situation and/or conditions under which the people being held responsible work.

Since it is extremely unlikely that any one individual will embody all the skills and virtues required to make a given decision, the idea of shared decision making should be considered. All decisions should be viewed as means rather than ends. Furthermore, since decisions are essentially temporary and experimental, the greater the input into the decision-making process the greater the chance for success. After all, the collective skills, virtues, and experiences of a group are logically better than those of any one person. The collective acceptance of the responsibilities of educating all students by a school system should not preclude individuals from sharing in the decisions to help all students find success.

A fifth consideration in the restruc-

*"With authority, responsibility and accountability, all of which grow pride, we can make it happen — without it, I am frightened for our schools of the future."*

—A principal

turing of schools is *research*. Change for the sake of change may not produce the desired results. Therefore, school reform efforts should be consciously and purposefully grounded in research. Practices documented as effective should be incorporated into the educational process. Similarly, practices that have been found to be harmful and ineffective should be rejected and/or discarded.

This is not to say that empirical research findings should serve as the sole basis for restructuring schools. Rather than just imitating and implementing the work of others, we will need to consider the generalizability of research findings from one situation to another. Keeping this in mind, the process should proceed in a thoughtful manner with collaborative participation from administrators, teachers, parents, and community members.

Nonetheless, the ensuing discussions of these individuals should revolve around research-based information about state-of-the-art practices. Equipped with the knowledge of what works, they will need to assess the implications of change for their district, their schools, and their students. Based upon these assessments, individuals involved in school reform will need to plan, to experiment with proposals for change, to engage in action research, and to reflect upon the effectiveness of the proposals based upon their implementation at the local level.

To implement these reform efforts will require *resources*, a sixth factor to be considered in restructuring our school systems. If schools are to travel where schools have never gone, developing a plan and wishing it so will not necessarily make it so. Education is a human enterprise and it is labor intensive. Although great strides have been made in the use of technology as teaching tools, the educational process will still only be able to travel as far as the available human resources will allow.

The resources needed to implement educational reform go beyond fiscal resources to include human resources and time. Policy makers from the national level on down to the local level are quick to point out the amount of money expended on education. Without debating the issue of equity in terms of either the manner in which education is funded at the local level or the distribution of these resources from district to district, many people view education merely as an expenditure rather than as an investment in human capital for the future.

Gross figures can be misleading, however. An international comparison of spending on education for grades K–12 in 1985 indicated that Americans ranked 14th out of 16 industrialized nations as a percentage of Gross Domestic Product (GDP). These figures make it clear that many nations invest a larger share of their wealth in the education of their youth than we do. In addition, the discrepancies in per-pupil expenditures within the U.S. are unmatched by any nation with a centralized educational system. While the fiscal resources available to improve education are important, they are by no means the only resources that

> *"We need to stay current with what really works and we need to experiment if we are going to improve."*
>
> —A principal

need to be considered.

The human resources of a school system are the heart and soul of the educational process. Yet, in many instances, perhaps most, they are allocated in a manner similar to supplies, materials, and equipment. There are rules for allocating staff, whether by mandate, certification, contractual agreement, policy, or a combination of these factors, which are frequently based upon a formula of some type. Once the staff is in place, little consideration is given by the school system to designing, coordinating, and implementing an ongoing professional development program based on the needs of administrators and teachers, or the high-priority student outcomes. Ironically, school systems miss a golden opportunity to demonstrate that learning is in fact a lifelong process. By failing to invest in the human capital of schools, we may be promoting the very status quo that the reform efforts are attempting to overcome.

Another human resource that schools need to reengage in the education process is that of the family—the social capital of society. While the Norman Rockwell family of the 1950s is rare in today's society, students do spend more time in the presence of adults outside school and in their homes on any given day than they do with administrators and teachers in school. We will need to reassess our present notions of parent involvement and the means by which we engage parents in the educational process. It is essential that we regain the confidence, the cooperation, and the active involvement of adults in the process of student learning if we are to achieve the fundamental purpose of schooling.

The process of student learning occurs over a period of time and it occurs at varying rates for different students. Administrators and teachers alike will rank time as one of their most precious resources. It is perhaps the single most valuable resource we have, after money. But, we have relegated this resource to that of a constant with regard to student learning, i.e., 180 days of school per year, 6–7 hours of school per day, X-number of minutes of instruction per class per day, etc. Not only do these self-imposed time constraints fly in the face of what we know about the ability of students to learn and student learning styles, they render the use of school facilities and equipment essentially unused a majority of the calendar year and a vast majority of the day.

Fiscal resources, human capital, social capital, and time are available to schools in finite quantities. On the one hand, administrators and teachers will express concern that these resources are insufficient to accomplish their mission. However, the question of how these resources are utilized is rarely addressed. Any discussion of the resources needed to restructure schools should also include how effectively and efficiently we make use of the resources currently available to education.

A seventh factor to consider in school restructuring is the *result* of the educational process. While these results

> *"Sure money is important, but I need more time and my staff needs more time. There just doesn't seem to be enough of either of these resources."*
>
> —A principal

are a consequence of the implementation and interaction of each of the factors outlined above, they manifest themselves in the education of the students served. The desire to improve student learning should be the primary consideration for altering those factors. We need to be sure that our primary motivation in school improvement efforts is the improvement of student learning conditions, rather than adult working conditions.

However, student outcome measures, by themselves, will not lead to the improvement of educational results. Student learning is the product of the quality of services they received, but the results do not directly measure the quality of those ongoing services. Thus, while we will need to clearly establish the nature and quality of expected student outcomes in a restructured school, we will also need to focus on nature and quality of the intermediate steps related to student and staff performance that will lead to improved student learning.

Equally important to the results of the educational process are the methods by which they are assessed. To this end, the National Council on Education Standards and Testing has recommended the development of high standards and a system of assessments measuring the degree to which they are attained. They have also concluded that the standards should contain an overarching vision statement, content standards, student performance standards, school delivery standards, and system performance standards. Once the standards have been established, multiple forms of assessment—rather than a single test—would need to be developed with particular attention being paid to the reliability, validity, and fairness of the assessment instruments.

Unless we can develop, implement, and effectively communicate the performance standards and the student achievement results to students, parents, community members, teachers, and administrators, our requests for the scarce public resources needed to deliver our services will continue to be difficult at best. Unless we can demonstrate and justify our needs, the basic line of "trust me" will only go so far, as we are finding out.

> *"Student outcomes drive everything. We are at the watershed period in the history of education where we can move beyond our present assessment practices which rely primarily on easily measurable student objectives to practices which will help us improve what we are doing."*
>
> —A principal

## One Size Does Not Fit All

In our present-day pluralistic society, it is remarkable to think that any one remedy could address the diverse and changing needs of all the people. They are all different. They come with a variety of characteristics and behaviors that change. They have different strengths, weaknesses, virtues, and needs. Does one size fit all? Consider why Heinz made 57 varieties, or why Baskin-Robbins made 31 flavors. So, why should we believe that education, which is a human enterprise, could have found the secret to meeting the educational needs of all people by developing the "one-best system"?

Look inside the new and old structures, look beneath the veneer, and the American public school systems are essentially the same. While some have newer and fancier toys, bigger and better bells and whistles, they are all cut essentially from the same mold. They follow the same basic school calendar, school day, etc. Most schoolwork is divided into classes that meet for uniform periods of time, distinct and apart from other classes. If students successfully complete the requirements, generally established by the individual teacher, they earn a specified number of credits toward graduation. Yet, the reality is that within the "one-best system" there is a great deal of diversity within each school, within each discipline, and within each classroom.

In spite of these differences, which are manifested in the culture of a school, there is a tendency to equate individual students, schools, and school systems based upon nebulous results in which there is generally a low correlation between the actual teaching-learning process and the reported results. As a consequence, these results are of little use other than to identify global trends over a period of time. Unfortunately, in most instances these results in the "one-best system" are used to sort, label, and rank students, schools, and districts, rather than as a means of assessing how well we are achieving the fundamental purpose of our schools.

If we truly want to improve the effectiveness of our educational system, then we will need to look at the difference between the present productivity and the desired results of this human enterprise from both a macro and micro perspective. If we are not achieving the desired outcomes for all students, then the question becomes, why continue to perpetuate the same system with only cosmetic alterations to existing practices or programs? Why continue to promote the myth of the "one-best system"? Why continue to reward many of our students for time-in-seat (social promotion), rather than actual achievement? Why continue to reward our school personnel in step-like fashion based upon longevity rather than productivity?

If a fundamental restructuring of education is needed, it will need to be as diverse as the society it serves and responsive to the changing needs of society. One size will not fit all. To produce a substantial, results-oriented systemwide change that will endure, we will need to develop shared understandings derived from individual and group values and beliefs. Therefore, talk of school reform and restructuring will need to be based upon changes in the culture of schools, rather than just changes in organizational or programatic structures.

> "*Even though we all have different interests, likes, and dislikes, schools are designed to treat everyone the same.*"
>
> —*A principal*

The cultural changes in the seven "R's" will not come easily. They will be threatening and risky to many, if not most, individuals. But, unlike tinkering with the existing system, these cultural changes do hold the promise of truly altering the educational process.

# References

Chubb, J. E., and Moe, T. M. *Politics, Markets, and America's Schools.* Washington, D.C.: The Brookings Institution, 1990.

Coleman, J. S. *Policy Perspectives: Parental Involvement in Education.* Washington, D.C.: U.S. Department of Education, 1991.

Corbett, H. D. *On the Meaning of Restructuring.* Philadelphia: Research for Better Schools, 1990.

Covey, S. R. *The 7 Habits of Highly Effective People.* New York: Simon & Schuster Inc., 1989.

Dentzer, E., and Wheelock, A. *Locked In/Locked Out: Tracking and Placement in Boston Public Schools.* Boston: Massachusetts Advocacy Center, 1990.

Duttwiler, P. C., and Mutchler, S. E. *Organizing the Educational System for Excellence: Harnessing the Energy of People.* Austin, Tex.: Southwest Educational Development Laboratory, 1990.

Elmore, R. F. "Choice in Public Education." Center for Policy Research in Education, 1986.

Fleming, D. S. *Decision Making in Restructuring Schools.* Andover, Mass.: The Regional Laboratory for Educational Improvement of the Northeast & Islands, 1990.

Hodgkinson, H. "Reform Versus Reality." *Phi Delta Kappan* 73 (1): 9–16.

Jacobson, S. L., and Conway, J. A. *Educational Leadership in an Age of Reform.* White Plains, N.Y.: Longman, 1990.

Kanter, R. M. *When Giants Learn to Dance.* New York: Simon & Schuster, Inc., 1990.

Kanter, R. M. *The Change Masters.* New York: Simon & Schuster, Inc., 1983.

Kearns, D. T., and Doyle, D. P. *Winning the Brain Race: A Bold Plan to Make Our Schools Competitive.* San Francisco: ICS Press, 1988.

Mojkowski, C. *Developing Leaders for Restructuring Schools: New Habits of Mind and Heart.* Reston, Va.: National Association of Secondary School Principals, 1990.

Mojkowski, C. *An Improving School: A Framework and Approach.* Cranston, R.I.: Rhode Island Educational Leadership Academy, 1989.

NASSP Commission on Restructuring. *A Leader's Guide to School Restructuring.* Reston, Va.: National Association of Secondary School Principals, 1992.

National Council on Education Standards and Testing. *Raising Standards for American Education.* Washington, D.C.: U.S. Government Printing Office, 1992.

Rasell, M. E., and Mishel, L. *Shortchanging Education.* Washington, D.C.: Economic Policy Institute, 1990.

Schlecty, P. C. *Schools for the Twenty-First Century.* San Francisco: Jossey-Bass, 1990.

Sizer, T. R. *Horace's Compromise: The Dilemma of the American High School.* Boston: Houghton-Mifflin, 1984.

Spady, W. G. "Organizing for Results: The Basis of Authentic Restructuring and Reform." *Educational Leadership* 46 (2): 4–8.

Spady, W. G., and Marshall, K. J. "Beyond Traditional Outcome-Based Education." *Educational Leadership* 49 (2): 67–72.

Warner, D., ed. *A View From the Inside: Addressing the Impediments to Shared Decision Making.* Albany, N.Y.: Leadership in Educational Administration Development Center, 1989.

Wiggins, G. "Standards, Not Standardization: Evoking Quality Student Work." *Educational Leadership* 48 (5): 18–25.

# CHAPTER 4

# How and When Can Schools Reform?

Our educational system must possess the flexibility and adaptability to respond quickly to the changing needs of society and the clients it serves. This will require that we examine the existing culture of our school systems. At the heart of this culture are the beliefs and attitudes that drive the system and the values that the individuals within the system share. Such a task will not be easy.

First, we must recognize that schools and school systems are not closed systems. Since we continuously interact with the surrounding social and political system, we must make provisions to include meaningful dialog with both the public and private agencies of these systems. We can no longer cut off communication with the community we serve by sending the message, "Don't worry, we'll take care of the education of our students," that has characterized past school improvement efforts.

> *"A plan must be developed to put a collaborative decision-making model in place for all school decisions which affect teaching and learning. The plan should include orientation and learning sessions about teamwork methods and shared decision making."*
>
> —A principal

> *"Involving people throughout the school in decisions makes their successful implementation more likely."*
>
> —A principal

Second, the traditional top-down model of school improvement that pitted experts against practitioners and suggested that knowledge comes from experts and is doled out to practitioners, will need to be revamped. Given the interaction of society and schools, a new top-down, bottom-up model should include a cooperative collaboration from practitioners, experts, community agencies, and the community. Within such a model, schools would be viewed as imperfect institutions that are continually growing and changing, rather than as places in need of repair. Instead of focusing on the implementation of "the" solution, the focus can be turned to the problem itself, with practitioners and experts actively engaged in reflecting on a problem and its potential solutions. If all parties are not active participants in the solutions of the problems in education, then in all likelihood they will continue to be part of the problems.

School-site management provides the philosophical basis for such a model. It is based upon the fundamental beliefs that those most closely affected by decisions in our schools ought to play a significant role in making those decisions, and that educational reform efforts are most effective and long-lasting when carried out by people who feel a sense of ownership and responsibility for the process. However, it does not mandate "a" solution nor "a" structure for the school improvement effort. Rather, school-site management is an eclectic process that can be molded and shaped to address the diversity of student needs in individual schools. At the same time, the individual school must cooperate with other schools in the district to achieve the overarching vision of the school district.

While a school-site management process may pose great promise for decentralizing the bureaucratic system, we should recognize that it will not—nor is it intended to—lead to the total demise of all centralized functions. For example, collective bargaining and financing of the district schools are functions that are more appropriately conducted from a centralized position than at the individual school level. These functions are based upon the expectations and the overall vision for the district that establishes the parameters within which the schools must operate. Therefore, while the purpose of school-site management is to create building level autonomy, it still must be achieved within the dictates of the larger system.

If schools are to be granted substantive decision-making authority over curriculum, personnel, and resources, consideration must be given to existing policies that impede the process. Furthermore, commitments to support the process should be given by all the potential actors, to include allowances and plans for the inevitable period of organizational trial and error.

The foundation of the school-site management model is the shared decision-making process of the school-improvement TEAM (Together Everyone Achieves More). Ground rules for the selection of the TEAM members and for the shared decision-making process within the school should be carefully established. In turn, these ground rules will need to fit within the context of the overall vision for the district. What types of questions and problems are suitable for consideration in the shared decision-making process? What procedures will be agreed upon for making decisions? What type of information and feedback will be provided to TEAM members, to other district schools, to district officials, and to the community? Will the school boards, central office, superintendent, and teacher unions formulate and adopt policy statements supporting the shared decision-making process of the school-improvement TEAMs? Will all parties be willing to waive general and specific rules, policies, and/or contractual provisions that will seriously impede the function of the TEAM? Will the participants be provided with training in team building, group dynamics, problem-solving techniques, and decision-making strategies?

Given the structural inflexibility of the traditional industrial model of governance and the inefficiency of the hierarchical decision making in the typical bureaucratic system, the eclectic approach of school-site management has capabilities that the "one-best system" cannot promise. Vesting decision-making authority in those individuals who interact directly with students on a daily basis promises to increase the effectiveness of the school and student academic outcomes. It will also give school-based administrators and teachers the opportunity to make greater use of their individual and collective talents and initiative. Similarly, the opportunity for increased parental and community involvement in the direct operation of the school will foster improved home-school relations. This factor has been identified in the effective schools literature as a positive influence on student achievement.

*"If change is to take place it will happen between the principal, the students, and the teachers, not the school board and superintendent."*
—*A principal*

*"School structures and routines must be viewed as flexible tools to create the conditions for students and teachers to engage in authentic intellectual development."*
—*A principal*

feedback mechanisms, most of the necessary human resources for school improvement are already present in the school itself. Thus, the primary assistance that policy makers and the central office can offer is the opportunity for the school-improvement TEAM to release the potential of a school's human capital.

Within each school, the TEAM will need to focus their efforts toward two distinct ends. First, school improvement efforts must address the needs of the client of the educational enterprise—the student. While many individuals will openly bemoan the fact that the students of today have changed, that they aren't what they used to be, they are actually indicating their need to change. A look at the demographic and social characteristics of students clearly indicates that they are right. However, we must also recognize that they are the only students we have. Second, the TEAM will need to develop a means of integrating the services of people who share a common purpose within a common school culture. This internal social contract will allow the TEAM to view themselves and other school personnel as cooperative problem solvers, not as technicians nor program administrators. To achieve these ends, the TEAM will need the authority to make decisions regarding curriculum, personnel, and resources from the perspective of what is going on to foster learning, what is going

## Administering CPR to the School Culture

Despite the potential and the responsive advantages of the school-site management process, tension between school-level autonomy and systemwide uniformity will continue to present problems. In their effort to make all schools within their purview more effective, policy makers will continue to be tempted to mandate actions they feel will achieve that goal. However, because education is based upon the relationships and the interactions of people; the knowledge, skills, and experience of administrators and teachers; and, the personal growth and development of people based upon on to deter learning, and, what they can do to help.

A fundamental concern of the TEAM should be to develop and implement the curriculum not only in the school, but also within the larger context of the district, the state, and the information society. The questions to be addressed transcend specific procedures, curricula, and timetables to emphasize education in its broadest sense—the development of the whole student. Does the curriculum induce values, influence attitudes, and integrate diverse sources of knowledge to mold students into responsible, productive adults? Is the curriculum broad and adaptable enough to ensure that the rigorous educational standards do not lock certain students out of opportunities to learn higher thinking skills and access to high-status knowledge? Does the curriculum balance the transmission of facts and low-order skills with a focus on the integration of thematic content across disciplines? What is the effect of the "Carnegie Unit" on the integration of the curriculum across disciplines? Are "basic skills" defined to include logical reasoning and analysis, problem solving, and creative thinking for all students? Are there mechanisms to coordinate the curriculum between schools and provide for the smooth transition of students between educational levels and schools? Does the curriculum focus on instructional strategies that are successful with heterogeneous classes? Does the curriculum support plans designed to reduce skill disparities among all students?

> "*Establish clearly the basic belief in the purpose of the school and use that belief to guide all actions, even hiring practices.*"
>
> —A principal

These questions and others will pose a number of problems and a number of new opportunities for curriculum development. If the curriculum represents the selection from all available knowledge and skills that society values, then all students must be guaranteed access to that knowledge and those skills. The traditional curriculum guide, which in most cases was centrally developed, may be the simplest means for conveying the adopted curriculum to all the schools and individuals within a district. However, if the taught curriculum is the means teachers use to deal with individual student needs, then curricular decision making by the practitioners at the school site makes sense. On the other hand, sifting through the knowledge explosion of the information society will require the ongoing cooperation and collaboration between curriculum experts and practitioners to produce a constantly evolving curriculum.

The second fundamental concern for the TEAM involves personnel. While the individuals who deliver the services of the educational enterprise are unquestionably the keys to the success of the school, the issue of school personnel will also unquestionably be one of the most sensitive that the TEAM will face. Teacher unions concerned with the welfare of their membership and school boards, central office personnel, and superintendents, who view personnel decisions as functions of their respective roles, may view school-site personnel decisions as potentially troublesome. However, to improve the effectiveness of schools, teachers who differ from one another in ability, interests, and experience must internalize the mission of the school and form a unified school culture. If this does not occur, then the school personnel will run the risk of being a group of individuals who just happen to be assigned to the same work site.

The primary personnel questions the TEAM must grapple with will include the selection, professional development, and support for practitioners that will allow them to foster the learning of all students. How can the TEAM work collaboratively with the school board, the central office, the superintendent, and the teachers' union to consider the district and the school priorities in selecting individuals for positions in the school who will best meet those priorities? Can they develop and implement a means of nurturing and supporting a positive school culture between all the practitioners and individuals who deal with the school? Can they develop and implement mentor programs for new teachers and peer coaching for experienced teachers that will promote collaborative learning between all practitioners? Can they establish ongoing professional development programs that will move beyond the typical inservice training, aimed at improving what the practitioners are already doing, and cause them to think and work differently? Can the TEAM create a culture that promotes practitioners who are conscious of, concerned about, and active in defining the

> "*As an individual, I endorse and support the concept of school-site management. Greater decision making authority is needed at the site level and the building personnel need to be involved with the expenditures and associated with the applications of site-based budgeting.*"
>
> —*A principal*

very nature of the profession, its purpose, and its goals, rather than pragmatic managers and technicians? Can the TEAM sustain their own capabilities and commitment to shared decision making when confronted with opposition from new TEAM members, new board members, a new superintendent, a new principal, and/or new teachers?

The responses to these and other personnel questions touch upon organizational dynamics and provide the basis for an evolving system. As the personnel become more involved in their own destiny, they will be less likely to become stuck in the rut of the status quo. They will also be given the opportunity to attain the status of a true professional.

The procurement of resources necessary to implement and support the curricular and personnel decisions is the third fundamental concern of the TEAM. Based upon the identification of problems and the resources needed to solve them, the TEAM should have the authority to make decisions regarding how the resources will best be allocated within the school. They must also act as advocates for additional resources on behalf of the school.

The questions of resource allocation will not be easy, given the finite availability of resources to schools and the seemingly infinite demand for them. Furthermore, the TEAM should not confine its deliberations solely to the allocation of fiscal resources. Will all students, especially marginal students or those who have a history of school failure, be provided with the support they will need to succeed? Can adopted curricular standards be met by all students within the timeframes of the traditional school year, the established school day, and/or the established school schedule? Will new curricular directions be developed and implemented? Will the established curriculum be modified? Will portions of the curriculum be eliminated? What will the implications of these curricular actions be for the associated supplies, materials, and equipment? for the school facilities? for the addition or reduction of staff? for time allocations? for technical assistance? How will priorities be established for the allocation of resources? Ultimately, the budgetary process at the school level will send a clear message to all the interested parties of exactly what the priorities of the TEAM are in terms of curriculum and student learning.

> *"The fact remains that all aspects of what is done in schools should be driven by the achievement of agreed upon student outcomes. Student outcomes, authentically assessed, should focus on the use of one's mind and the key concepts. Student outcomes, which are agreed upon, set the stage for a professional development plan, school schedule, learning experiences, reporting to the community, etc."*
>
> —A principal

## Operational Success — Reassessing the Means and the Ends

Neither the quantifiable measures of student achievement, currently used in the typical top-down hierarchical model, nor the "bottom line," which is based upon fiscal and personnel input, will serve as an adequate assessment of the top-down, bottom-up form of school governance. Performance assessment must be built into the function of the TEAM and the outcomes of the educational enterprise, i.e., the process and the products. At the school level, TEAM members should devise clear and acceptable ways of assessing the progress of the school and the students toward the achievement of the fundamental purpose and the goals established for the school. Similarly, new means for evaluating the school district should be developed. These evaluation and assessment results, when properly conceived and reported, will be the key elements in building a results-oriented, self-regulating school culture within the parameters of the school district.

While assessing the quality and equity of educational opportunities and the ends of the educational process, i.e., student outcomes, will be paramount to determining the success of school-site management, that should not be the only criterion for success. The means of the shared decision-making process made in a school should also be assessed from time to time. Do all the TEAM members accept the responsibility for the TEAM, its vision and goals, its successes and its failures? Do they all have an opportunity to express their opinions freely? Do they attempt to find common ground when disagreements occur? Do they support a spirit of innovation, along with accountability, for the actions of the TEAM and all the members of the school community? Are decisions made and supported jointly by all TEAM members? Since student outcomes will be determined in large part by the curricular, personnel, and resource decisions of the TEAM, an assessment of the individual and collective decisions and the decision-making process will be essential.

The new procedures for evaluation and assessment in a top-down, bottom-up form of school governance will also require a form of shared accountability. In a hierarchical system, it is difficult to hold groups of people accountable. Generally, individuals are held accountable based upon their position within the system; i.e., superintendents are accountable for the operation of school districts, and principals are accountable for the operation of schools. However, in a top-down, bottom-up system, formal and informal networks of people tend to be the norm. These networks tend to be more horizontal than vertical; leadership tends to be based more on competence and interpersonal relations than on social or organizational rank; communications flow in all directions, sometimes simultaneously, rather than the traditional vertical "chain of command"; and power and control turn over more frequently and easily than in a bureaucracy. The adaptability of such a system is a function of the cooperative and collaborative relationships of the network members. If the shared decision-making model is accepted by all participants, then accountability by all participants is equally essential.

Similarly, new and authentic means of assessing individual and collective student outcomes must be developed to drive school improvement efforts. Can we de-

> "*We need to look at both the process and the product to determine how we are doing, otherwise we just rationalize the results in one way or another without ever really knowing why.*"
>
> —*A principal*

velop and implement procedures to assess how well the vision and goals of schools are being achieved? Will performance standards be developed and by whom? Can valid and reliable means of evaluating student performance be developed? How can criterion-referenced and norm-referenced assessments be used to improve the performance of practitioners? schools? school systems? How will this information be communicated? How will this information be used? Who will receive this information? These and other questions must be answered, lest we repeat the errors of the past. We cannot afford to declare that the operation was a success, but the client died. If the top-down, bottom-up reform of school governance is to succeed, all the participants in our educational enterprise must honestly report and accept the responsibility for the outcomes of the means and the ends, collectively.

Finally, how can these outcomes be used in terms of a reward system based upon productivity for the school, the school system, school officials, and practitioners? Most current systems reward individual performance monetarily based upon longevity in the system, the accumulation of degrees and/or credits earned, and the position within the system. While money is an incentive to do work, it is not an incentive to do work well or differently. On the contrary, doing a good job in the "one-best system" requires individuals to play by the established rules, to implement them as faithfully and effectively as possible, and to not "rock the boat." Such a system actually stifles creativity, originality, and innovations that could lead to school improvement. Most reward systems are not based upon any form of individual or collective recognition nor status for productivity. In spite of this, the current efforts by many individuals and groups of individuals to improve schools is one indication of the intrinsic motivation that many practitioners possess to promote student learning and their own professional development.

## The Principal and the Principles

The idea of shared decision making in the governance of schools is a notion that some principals find troubling. Others, however, will argue that such an idea is not new and that they have made it a practice to regularly involve teachers in decisions. In either case, the principal will undoubtedly be the key figure in fostering the relationships that will be necessary for effective shared decision making within the school.

A principal who becomes involved in school-site management will need to invite others to share the authority of the position and to accept the responsibilities as well. Such a principal will need to place the same trust in others that he or she expects in return. However, because so much of the technical and day-to-day

---

*"Teacher empowerment and school-based decision making must never be considered threats to administrative authority, but considered to be issues that contribute to the successful operation of schools everywhere."*

—*A principal*

*"I think most good principals use some form of school-based management. This is really not a new concept."*

—*A principal*

---

operational knowledge of the school is concentrated in the practitioners in a school, the open acknowledgment of the informal authority that they currently exercise as part of shared decision making may serve to build such trust. On the other hand, individuals who routinely rely on the authority and power of their position to compel others to act will serve to maintain the status quo of the hierarchical system. As such, the authoritarian principal will find it difficult, if not impossible to establish the type of school culture needed to implement shared decision making. So, how does the role of the principal mesh with the principles of school-site management?

First, the role of the principal must become that of a change agent. It will require a great deal of interaction with practitioners—informing, motivating, facilitating, and leading—if the changes are to succeed. They will need to develop specific skills that enable them to form cooperative teams, where individuals existed; to coordinate the efforts of multi-teams while maintaining a dual-focus, i.e., the common culture and purpose of the school while encouraging the autonomy necessary for innovation and to provide the support and encouragement needed to build consensus rather than relying on the sole decision makers in the school.

Second, principals will need to balance their seemingly conflicting roles as managers—the maintenance of stability and predictable—with the demands of instructional leadership—the destabilizing and unpredictable impact of change. Furthermore, these efforts will be compounded by the demands to maintain a balance between the coordination of the individual and group dynamics of the school-site TEAM with the individual needs and demands of students, parents, teachers, and the central office. Nonetheless, the overall view of the school from the perspective of a principal makes him or her the key resource in the school in terms of curriculum, personnel issues, and resources.

While the influence of the authoritarian principal is directly observable, the leadership of principals involved in shared decision making is only indirectly seen. Sharing in the decision-making process may imply to some that the authority of the principal is diminished. However, many others feel that the authority and responsibility of the principal actually expands in three directions, i.e., more direct involvement in the school programs, more direct involvement in governance, and a higher level of responsibility in district decision making. Furthermore, since the principal's sphere of communication is greater and more direct, his or her influence in the district may actually increase.

Shared decision making at the school-site level calls for effective leadership, research-based knowledge of the profession, the promulgation of a common school culture, and experience in the day-to-day process of teaching and learning. The ultimate form that it takes in any given school will be a function of these factors. The principal and the principles of school-site management and shared decision making, when adopted and implemented, can lead to a restructuring of the "one-best system." Finally, a top-down, bottom-up structure of school governance can provide a vehicle for the educational enterprise that meets the diverse needs within a school district. It fosters innovation and coordination within and between schools, which is more effective and efficient than a top-down model. It is more flexible and adaptable than a hierarchical bureaucratic system, and it is more responsive to the changing information society than a relatively closed system. All in all, it promotes lifelong learning in all the individuals associated with our schools.

# References

Block, P. *The Empowered Manager: Positive Political Skills at Work.* San Francisco: Jossey-Bass, 1991.

Chubb, J. E., and Moe, T. M. *Politics, Markets, and America's Schools.* Washington, D.C.: The Brookings Institution, 1990.

Clune, W. H., and White, P. A. *School-Based Management: Institutional Variation, Implementation, and Issues for Further Research.* New Brunswick, N.H.: Center for Policy Research in Education, 1988, pp. 19–23.

Conley, S. C., and Bacharach, S. B. "From School-Site Management to Participatory School-Site Management." *Phi Delta Kappan* 71 (7): 539–44.

Dentzer, E., and Wheelock, A. *Locked In/Locked Out: Tracking and Placement in Boston Public Schools.* Boston: Massachusetts Advocacy Center, 1990.

Drucker, P. F. *The New Realities.* New York: Harper & Row, 1990.

Duttweiler, P. C., and Mutchier, S. E. *Organizing the Educational System for Excellence: Harnessing the Energy of People.* Austin, Tex.: Southwest Educational Development Laboratory, 1990.

English, F. W. "School-Site Management." *The Practitioner* 16 (2): 1–6.

English, F. W., and Hill, J. C. *Restructuring: The Principal and Curriculum Change.* Reston, Va.: National Association of Secondary School Principals, 1990.

Finn, C. E., Jr. "Toward Strategic Independence: Nine Commandments for Enhancing School Effectiveness." *Phi Delta Kappan* 65 (8): 518–24.

Harsen, B. J. *School Improvement Councils: A Guide to Effectiveness.* Columbia, S.C.: The School Council Assistance Project, 1989, pp.15–26.

Hill, P. T.; Foster, G. E.; and Gendler, T. *High Schools with Character.* Santa Monica, Calif.: The RAND Corporation, 1990.

Jacobson, S. L., and Conway, J. A. *Educational Leadership in an Age of Reform.* White Plains, N.Y.: Longman, 1990.

Jenkins, K. "Metaphor and Mindset for Educational Leadership." *Educational Forum* 2 (1988): 143–51.

Kennedy, K. J. "School-Based Curriculum Development as a Policy Option for the 1990s: An Australian Perspective." *Journal of Curriculum and Supervision* 2 (1992): 180–95.

Kriegel, R. J. *If It Ain't Broke . . . BREAK IT!* New York: Warner Books, Inc., 1991.

Machiavelli, N. *The Prince.* New York: Mentor Books, 1952.

Mojkowski. C. *An Improving School: A Framework and Approach.* Cranston, R.I.: Rhode Island Educational Leadership Academy, 1989.

Mojkowski, C., and Fleming, D. S. *School-Site Management: Concepts and Approaches.* Cranston, R.I.: Rhode Island Educational Leadership Academy, 1988.

Pierce, L. C. "School Based Management." *Oregon School Study Council Bulletin* 10 (1980): 6–21.

Schlecty, P. C. *Schools for the Twenty-First Century.* San Francisco: Jossey-Bass, 1990.

Sirotnik, K. A., and Clark, R. W. "School-Centered Decision Making and Renewal." *Phi Delta Kappan* 69 (9), pp. 660–64.

Thomas, M. D. "Are We Really Serious About Reform?" *Education Week* XI (22), p. 33.

Toffler, A. *Power Shift.* New York: Bantam Books, 1990.

Warner, D., ed. *A View from the Inside: Addressing the Impediments to Shared Decision Making.* Albany, N.Y.: Leadership in Educational Administration Development Center, 1989.

White, M. A. "Educating in the Information Age." *Educators Around the World Share Their Vision of a Design for School Year 2000.* Kansas City: Mid Continent Regional Educational Laboratory 1990, pp. 11–13.

Willoughby, S. S. *Mathematics Education for a Changing World.* Alexandria, Va.: Association for Supervision and Curriculum Development, 1990.

# CHAPTER 5

# Who Will Lead School Reform?

great deal has been written about management and leadership. We have all heard the statement that managers do things right, and leaders do the right things. Yet, both are essential to the successful operation of schools. Managerial activities tend to be impersonal, dealing with things and routines. They include the day-to-day mundane "to do" lists and attention to the fundamental routines that provide the foundation for a successful, self-sustaining enterprise. While less than exciting, for the most part, they are necessary. On the other hand, leadership activities deal with people.

In our schools, good managers are technically competent in getting things done in an efficient manner when directed to do so, and know how to solve problems. These people tend to be task oriented and reliable; they provide stability and predictability to the school. They also tend to maintain the status quo. However, those individuals who are considered to be leaders in our schools

> *"It is not a question of whether or not principals can be instructional leaders, they must be instructional leaders."*
>
> —A principal

> *"Instructional leadership must be our primary function."*
>
> —A principal

do not just complete tasks, they constantly seek to understand why they are dealing with a specific task, routine, or problem. They tend to have a vision of their ideal for the school and question if their actions and activities are on a course that will lead them there. They look for the routines and problems that cause them to stray off course and take corrective action. They are the change agents in the school.

So, who are the managers and leaders in the school? To one degree or another, all school personnel are both managers and leaders. They all have certain managerial functions they must perform to promote student learning. They all have some sort of vision for the ideal purpose for the school and the students it serves. And, they all have a basic sense of what is right and wrong for the school and the students. Consider the countless times that teachers, custodians, and secretaries take the initiative to identify problems and take action to improve the school. However, if a single individual in our schools had to be identified who will bring about the changes in education that will be necessary in the next century, it would be the principal.

Can a principal balance the managerial demands of the job with the leadership needs of the school? Can the principal maintain stability and calm within the context of change? Can the principal reconcile the pressures and forces from outside the school with those from within the school? Can the principal keep the ship afloat and on course? Finally, what would such a person look like and be like?

## Changes and Cows

There is little merit in opposing change. It will happen with or without our consent. Changes in society may be even more unpredictable than the weather. We know changes will occur and in some cases actually want them to occur. But we can never be exactly sure just when, where, how, nor why they will occur. Just as changes in the winds will blow a ship off course unless corrections are made, so too will the changes in the information society continue to create the need for changes in our schools. How can we prepare for the inevitable in our schools when we don't know what the inevitable will be? How can we prepare for the extent that the changes in society will have on our schools? Who is in the best position to answer these questions in the school?

Principals will need to use all their senses to gather first-hand information from a variety of sources. To accomplish this, they will need to keep their hands on the pulse of the school, the district, and the community. They will have to observe and listen intently to what others have to say, regardless of their perspective on a topic; to feel what people are not saying

*"Principals need to be very perceptive, use good judgment, and possess extensive general knowledge."*
—A principal

to catch the scent of change; to envision the ideal while looking at reality; to maintain the long-term view while dealing with the short term to keep a focus on the whole while focusing on the particular and to interpret and process an ocean of information into workable knowledge that will foster student learning. They will need to be master generalists in terms of the development of curriculum, human capital, and resources. The knowledge that a principal will need to possess is akin to that of the river boat pilot described by Mark Twain:

Two things seem pretty apparent to me. One was, that in order to be a pilot, a man had got to learn more than any one man ought to be allowed to know; and the other was, that he must learn it all over again in a different way every 24 hours.

While principals cannot be all knowing and all things to all people at all times, they frequently attempt to fill this unrealistic role. The frustration they feel in attempting to respond to a variety of demands often clouds their efforts and results in their failure to see the forest for the trees. They may be unable to identify the need for and the forces of change in the big picture if they are focusing on an individual frame. In some cases, those needs and forces may come from within the school, while in other cases, they come from sources external to the school. Typically, principals respond using fixed outlooks, methods, and rules for dealing with known and recurring situations. They fail to recognize that their own standard operating procedure and that of the "one-best system" may prevent them from looking at new information and knowledge from new perspectives. In essence, they may have allowed conventional practice to attain the status of a "sacred cow" that cannot be altered or changed. Perhaps it is the "sacred cows" that we have created or allowed to be created, our own traditional way of thinking, and/or our personal procedures and practices that create barriers to change. Perhaps it is the hierarchical system that has convinced us that all power and our well-being come from the outside and that our success depends on obedience and measuring up to the policies and requirements of others.

While teachers will bemoan their lack of "power" and "control" within the public school system, principals know they are caught between two general layers of the bureaucratic hierarchy—the central office and the teacher unions. They feel constrained by the policies and demands from above and the contractual obligations from below. As a result, they may think that their ability to create change is severely limited by a system in need of change. Ironically, while the traditional school system has relegated principals to managerial roles (while asking for leadership), the reality is that the system needs the leadership of good principals more than good

> ## "*Principals must have a great sense of purpose and a huge sense of humor.*"
>
> —A principal

principals need the system. Therefore, perhaps principals should spend less time worrying about the system controlling what happens to them, and focus their attention on controlling their own destiny by changing the system.

Principals are in highly visible and pivotal positions within the school. They have access to many sources of information and people. How they use these resources will be determined by their leadership ability and will ultimately determine their ability to influence change within the school and the school district. Will principals respond to the variety of sources of information, or only respond to that information that has a direct bearing on a particular situation? Will they respond to the multi-modal and multi-dimensional origins of information in the traditional linear-sequential pattern of logical thinking, or develop multi-dimensional strategies that emphasize whole, interdependent systems of thinking? Will they seek to include all the human resources available to them in identifying discrepancies between what should be and what is, or shoulder the burden themselves? Will they seek to harness the collective energy and creativity of a team of people to address the discrepancies, or rely on their own skill and knowledge? Will principals seek to creatively interpret the rules of the system to foster change, or succumb to the maintenance function and the status quo of existing rules? Will they be satisfied to react to what is, or seek to create what will be?

To begin addressing these questions, principals will need to become more active in seeking out problems than reactive to identified problems, and more reflective in terms of their own actions and those of others than just prescriptive. Waiting for problems to surface is merely waiting for the inevitable. Yet, waiting ultimately inhibits the development of solutions. Problems may be described as discrepancies between what is and what should be that become untenable or unbearable to someone. When discrepancies reach the status of problems, people react with heightened emotions and look for solutions to be developed and implemented in a timely fashion. They expect the principal to reduce the difference between the actual and the ideal to an acceptable level. Time becomes the primary constraining factor in the problem-solving process.

On the other hand, if principals actively seek to identify discrepancies before they become problems, they will be in a position to define and redefine the situation, identify and analyze the forces that created the discrepancy, and develop a number of potential solutions. To many principals who feel they spend so much of their time reacting to problems, any suggestion that they actually look for problems might seem masochistic. However, identifying discrepancies before they become problems provides principals with opportunities to engage those individuals who will be most directly affected by the potential problems. These individuals will then have the chance to be part of the problem-solving process in an atmosphere relatively free from the emotions that accompany most problems. It also allows principals to be selective about which discrepancies they will deal with directly or indirectly and in what order they will deal with them.

Actively seeking and identifying potential problems is not a management function, but rather a leadership function. Furthermore, reflecting on seemingly smooth operations and the "sacred cows" associated with such operations is actually forward looking. Both problem finding and reflection are processes that principals will need to engage in and feel comfortable with. Principals who become comfortable with these processes will recognize the tentative nature of past successes, the opportunity to create future successes, and the inevitability of change.

## Clients, Conductors, and Cures

All the individuals in our school and associated with our schools are just that—individuals. Each individual brings to the school a variety and range of beliefs, likes and dislikes, skills and knowledge, that have been and are constantly influenced by others. We also need to recognize that these influences occur both during school hours and outside school hours. Together these characteristics and the interactions between people cultivate and form the unique holistic portrait we see as an individual. But, it is also a portrait of change and of potential.

Can we picture these changes in a positive light when cast into the sea of doubt that surrounds our society and our world? Can we see the potential that lies within each individual, even when that potential is hidden? Can we tolerate the failures that accompany growth and development? Do these questions go to the very heart of the teaching and learning process? Ask virtually any person about the general potential for change in any individual and they will usually re spond optimistically. However, when you ask this same question about specific individuals, the answers are likely to vary. How, then, can we reconcile the universal belief in the potential of all individuals with the pessimistic view of specific individuals? Can principals be the visionary change agents our pluralistic society needs?

If principals are to meet the demands of being a change agent, they need to possess an infectious optimism about teaching and learning, and convey their beliefs to students, parents, and teachers. They must ask themselves a number of questions.

• Do I model my own internalized optimism in my informal as well as formal communications? in my informal actions as well as formal actions in school? in all my interactions with people outside the school?

• Do I find ways to pay attention to what I really feel is important?

• Do I challenge those processes, procedures, and beliefs that do not foster student learning, based upon my ethical and moral values and philosophical principles?

Do I constantly scan the environment for new opportunities?

Am I willing to experiment and take risks?

Do I develop a mental picture of the future and inspire and strengthen the resolve of others to share this vision?

> *"Principals need to possess flexibility, sensitivity, organizational skills, and a 'big picture' perspective. They must express the basic value of students, parents, and staff; effectively communicate with them; and, demand that they be included in sharing decisions that affect them."*
>
> —A principal

> *"Principals have to be the keeper of the dream in the school and share a vision of excellence with everyone in the school."*
>
> —A principal

To achieve these ends, principals must be willing to put themselves on the line by setting the example for others and facilitating winning situations for everyone within the school, by recognizing the contributions of individuals toward the achievement of the vision, and by celebrating individual and collective achievements. In essence, principals need to be not only the keeper of the dream, but also the promoter of the dream to all people associated with the school.

Since student learning is the primary function of our schools, students will need to share the vision. Individual students will need to be the focus of our attention in schools rather than just segments of the school population, which tend to obscure the individual. Again, the principal needs to be reflective with regard to the clients of the educational process. Do I recognize the individual worth of each student, rather than just the brightest and the best? Do I celebrate minor as well as major student achievements? Do I champion the individual efforts of all students? Do I seek and find time to directly observe students in a wide variety of settings? to speak with and listen to a variety of students? to work directly with individual students? If principals are to work with teachers and parents to meet student needs, they should assist in identifying those needs, despite all the

*51*

managerial and bureaucratic demands with which they must deal. While the professional staff members of a school may serve at the pleasure of the school board, their professional function is to serve students. They are our clients, not the bureaucracy of the "one-best system."

In terms of serving our clients, principals are in the best position to observe the school from a global perspective with respect to curriculum, personnel, and resources. They are also in the best position to creatively orchestrate a blending of the various aspects of the teaching and learning process to meet the needs of individual clients. From their global view of the school, principals have opportunities on a daily basis to combine their various frames of reference with those of others and draw connections between ostensibly unrelated points of view to create new learning situations. However, they will need to consciously recognize the discrepancies, whether large or small, and to trust their sense to create new opportunities.

This role of the principal may be somewhat parallel to that of the conductor of a philharmonic orchestra. Just as the conductor needs to blend the sounds of the various instruments with the skills of the individual musicians to produce an artistic performance, so too must principals act as conductors in our schools. Drawing upon their knowledge and experience, principals need to pull together the various resources within the school to create harmony where dissonance was observed. However, both orchestras and schools are subject to constant changes that may produce new dissonance. Therefore, the conductor needs to keep a sharp ear tuned toward all sections of the orchestra, individually and collectively, to identify areas where adjustments are needed. An analogous statement could be made regarding the need for principals to keep their fingers on the pulse of the school. However, neither conductors nor principals can address an ill if they don't know they have it. In an orchestra, instruments need periodic tuning and musicians need to constantly refine their talents to create new and improved performances. Similarly, the dynamics of individuals and groups of people in our schools and society require that school leaders constantly refine their talents and those of others to meet the changing needs of students. Yet, while both the conductor and the principal need to perceive the ideal, identify potential ills, and initiate change, they must realize that it is ultimately the collective performance of others that leads to desired outcomes. Given this reality, it would seem to make more sense to work with people rather than working to change them.

## Coach or Cop

About one person in five has a baccalaureate degree in the U.S. today, and most of these people are working in our public schools. Therefore, principals have an opportunity to work with some of the most educated people in our country. As such, they should view and treat the teachers in a school as a community of professionals rather than a labor force. In turn, principals will need to view teachers as colleagues, rather than subordinates. By working with teachers to help them grow professionally, principals can foster student learning. In so doing, both principals and teachers become part of a teaching team.

Although this might seem like "pie in-the-sky" idealism to some, conside who depends upon whom within a school to effectively fulfill their respective visions? Teachers depend on principals and other teachers, and principals depend on teachers. It would seem only natural that they should work together in a collaborative and cooperative atmosphere of mutual trust and confidence free from suspicion. To identify the potential of teachers and students and provide growth opportunities and outlets for expressing these potentials, principals will need to function from a "coaching" frame of reference, rather than that of a "cop." They will need to work with all the members of the school community to identify discrepancies between what is and what should be, to share with them in their successes and failures, to help them focus on students as the clients of the educational process, and to actively communicate with all members of the school community.

While this is not to say that principals should never confront teachers or students, nor that teachers or students should never confront principals, the coaching perspective provides principals, teachers, and students with a growth mechanism that is constructive, consultative, helpful, and collegial. To this end, principals should reflect on their own behavior to determine if they are promoting the growth and development of teachers and students. Do I really believe that teachers, students, and principals can become a community of learners within the school? Do I constantly reinforce this belief in teachers and students through my actions as well as my words? Do I encourage and develop teamwork, confidence, and support for teachers and students? Do I model the belief that all individuals can perform to the best of their ability? that everyone can learn? that lifelong learning is a reality and not just a cliché? that I am willing to spend the necessary amount of time and available resources to assist them in their growth and development? Do I build trust and respect with teachers and students? Do I encourage them to experiment in their learning? Do I realize and communicate to others that today's failure is no more fatal than yesterday's success is permanent? Do I recognize that teaching and learning is a long-term process of becoming? If schools are to become communities of learners, then all members of the school community must become teachers and learners. We must all be prepared to address these questions, as well as many others; to seize the opportunities that present themselves and take the risks necessary to achieve new results; to overcome the fear of failure; and to create future learning opportunities.

Keeping in mind that everything

> "*I believe teachers are professionals and if I set the tone and direction for the school, they will carry this school forward.*"
>
> —A principal

> "*Leadership is releasing the energy of others, i.e., students and staff. The biggest challenge today is to inspire your staff. Put your emphasis on the positive. It is important to have the best teacher available in each classroom at all times.*"
>
> —A principal

worthwhile carries the risk of failure, we should consider that learning is a combination of trial and error. If we fail to act because there is a possibility that we might fail, we also deny ourselves an opportunity to succeed. Just think, the greatest hitters in the game of baseball, those enshrined in the baseball Hall of Fame, all failed to get hits on an average of 4 of every 10 times they batted. If we can recognize those baseball heroes as champions, even though their failure rate exceeded their success rate, why then do we fear failure in our schools? Why are we afraid of making mistakes? Making mistakes in school is not against the law. In fact, not making mistakes may be the biggest mistake of all. Mistakes allow a person to rethink, to reconceptualize, to formulate new strategies, and to learn. If we are to grow, to expand our knowledge of what is, to expand our vision of what could be, we must be willing to take risks.

However, we should also recognize that risk takers are neither wild nor crazy people. In contrast to the daredevil, risk takers do not take chances and are actually quite sane. They focus on what they can do, rather than what they can't do; they turn anxiety into anticipation; they change the question "what if?" into the declaration of "if...then"; and, they mentally prepare, prepare, and prepare. Their positive mental attitude allows them to overcome the distortion of fear to visualize themselves in action accomplishing their goal. Rather than policing the action of others, which is restrictive and regulatory in nature, we need to promote others to act. The lead-

ers in our schools should instill action mode beliefs in both teachers and students just as coaches cultivate a winning attitude in athletes by instilling in them the belief that they will succeed.

> "*A principal must be a facilitator and become a 'leader of leaders,' not just an instructional leader.*"
> —A principal

## Chaos, Calm, and Culture

How can we balance the need for change within a stable environment? How can we respect the diversity and rights of individuals and at the same time expect conformity in some areas for the good of all the members of the school community? How can we encourage freedom of expression on the one hand and impose restrictions on the other? How can we provide equal opportunities to all and expect and encourage individuals to take advantage of the existing opportunities to become all they can be? The answers to these questions manifest themselves in the culture of the school. This culture focuses on the behavioral patterns of the individuals who comprise the school community and the values, beliefs, and norms that define and sustain those patterns Principals, teachers, and students are strongly influenced by the morale, the mores, and the conscious and unconscious ways that things are done in their schools. They need to consciously reflec upon which practices promote learning which practices are undesirable or inef fective, and which practices have become the conventional modus operandi of th school.

Symbolically, principals reflect an shape the culture of schools. Who the are, what they do, what they attend to and what they reward are constantl watched by all members of the school community. Virtually any task, idea, or belief is likely to take on new meaning when principals demonstrate sincere concern. To move toward implementing their vision for the school, principals need to be aware of their influence in shaping the culture of the school.

Principals need to constantly monitor and identify the cultural dimensions of their job and the concrete things they can do, in concert with teachers, students, and community members to create a school culture that responds to the changing needs of all students. Do I understand the inner workings of the school's values and norms and reflect on their match with the overall vision for the school? Do I identify the norms, values, and beliefs I want to reinforce, as well as those I want to change? Do I make explicit commitments to change known to others? Do I work with all the stakeholders in the school to clarify the vision and purposes of the school? Do I reinforce the core values and norms of the school through my own actions? Do I highlight the priority of additional values and beliefs which are not prominent in the existing culture but which support the vision for the school? Do I regularly reassess the extent to which all members of the school community share the vision for the school? Do I evaluate the degree to which the school culture reinforces and supports the school's mission? In addressing these questions, principals will force themselves reflect on the reality of what is happening in their schools. In turn, staying in touch with what is really going on in the school is one of the best ways to force oneself to grow.

> "*Establish clear definitions of priorities for schools, and a strong commitment to the values that affect student learning — the output of the school process.*"
>
> —*A principal*

While dealing with the esoteric questions of the dream and the vision of the future, principals must also deal with the pragmatic realities of the present. Reaffirming both positions in a school often seems paradoxical; i.e., strategically planning for change, yet being resilient enough to recognize an unplanned opportunity when it presents itself; reconciling the elitist perspective within a pluralistic culture; providing discretion within mandates; providing transformational leadership while managing the day-to-day operation of the school; promoting individuality while fostering collegiality; nurturing those values and beliefs that pertain to the intangibles of quality while dealing with the quantifiable bottom-line; and maintaining a holistic perspective while dealing with a specific part. Principals need to become comfortable living in a state of continuous imbalance between the dream and reality. They must learn to tack between these two points on the compass to avoid the potential of allowing the school culture to drift into a state of chaos or becoming caught in the doldrums of the calm that frequently result in maintaining the status quo.

## Compendium and Commencement

As society beckons for changes in the educational system, various segments of public and private sectors of society are stepping forward to lead the charge. Upon closer inspection, however, most of these groups and individuals are merely pointing out directions or offering fragmented suggestions, but not sustained or coordinated leadership. So, the question still remains, who will be the leaders of educational reform in the next century?

The leadership that will be necessary to transform the potential energy of the current hierarchical and bureaucratic system into a dynamic and responsive system will come from many sources. No longer can we look solely to a person in a particular position to provide leadership nor can the "one-best system" isolate itself from the larger society it serves. Therefore, we must look for leadership outside and inside the system; we must look for leadership from the bottom up as well as from the top down; and we must look to shifting situational leadership as well as positional leadership. Regardless of where this leadership comes from, the leaders of educational reform must realize that the individual school will be the place of change.

The leaders of school reform must call people who understand the long-term needs of society to higher levels of performance. They will need to be courageous individuals who see themselves as change agents, who know what they believe in, who believe in people, and who are lifelong learners themselves. They must help individuals within the school community to move, in their thinking and their behavior, beyond the limits of their own experience. They will need to create self-managing and self-learning groups and invest in developing people.

> "*The principalship is the most invigorating, thrilling, important, and frustrating role in public education.*"
>
> —*A principal*

They must seek to identify and nurture potential leaders to ensure that the change process is systemwide, rather than dependent on any one individual. These leaders must possess knowledge, vision, and virtue. Without complementary degrees of each of these characteristics, these individuals may not be able to demonstrate the leadership that will inspire others to act.

The people in the best position to become the leaders in our schools are the principals. They are, or should be, at the hub of all school activities. They possess the global perspective for the school in terms of the vision, as well as managing the implementation of the vision. To assume this leadership, however, principals must be multifaceted and ambidextrous. They must learn to operate without the might of the hierarchy behind them; to operate with the highest ethical standards; to possess a sense of humor with a dose of humility that says there are always new things to learn; to work across functions and disciplines; to find synergies that multiply the value of the human resources of the school; to swim equally effectively downstream, upstream, and in the mainstream while staying on course and managing the dream; to embrace error as a means of growth and learning; to compete in a way that enhances rather than undercuts cooperation; to develop a respect for the process of implementation as well as the substance of what is implemented; to encourage reflective discourse; to encourage people to express dissent; to periodically take the pulse of the school culture; and to create strategic alliances and partnerships between the various constituencies within the school and between the public and private sectors of the community and the school. During this time, principals must exude their own personal optimism, confidence, and hope for the school.

Good principals have always recognized that they function professionally where the action is. In these trying and changing times, the public and private sectors of society need look no further than our schools for the leaders of the future. In fact, most principals would relish the chance to work with others to design and implement changes to the existing educational system. While there will be many new leaders in ongoing school improvement efforts, we can be sure one of them will be the school principal. Ask any student about the school, and he or she will probably tell you to ask the principal. The students know!

> *"Principals have to be the leaders for change."*
>
> —*A principal*

# References

Achilles, C. M., and Norris, C. "Vignette: Alas! A Report of a Non-Commission on Excellence in Leadership." *NFEAS Journal* 3 (1): 103–06.

Bennis, W. *On Becoming a Leader.* Reading, Mass: Addison-Wesley Publishing Co., 1989.

Deal, T. E., and Peterson, K. D. *The Principal's Role in Shaping School Culture.* Washington, D.C.: U.S. Department of Education, 1990.

Engel, M. "From B.C. to PC." *Educators Around the World Share Their Vision of a Design for School Year 2020.* Kansas City: Mid-Continent Regional Educational Laboratory, 1990, pp. 17–19.

English, F. W., and Hill, J. C. *Restructuring: The Principal and Curriculum Change.* Reston, Va.: National Association of Secondary School Principals, 1990.

Gainey, D. D. "Teacher Evaluation and Supervision for School Improvement: Myth or Reality?" *NASSP Bulletin,* March 1990.

Heider, J. *The Tao of Leadership.* New York: Bantam Books, 1985.

Jenkins, K. "Metaphor and Mindset for Educational Leadership." *Educational Forum* 52 (2): 143–51.

Kanter, R. M. *When Giants Learn To Dance.* New York: Simon & Schuster Inc., 1990.

Kreigel, R. J. *If It Ain't Broke ... BREAK IT!* New York: Warner Books, 1991.

Kouzes, J. M., and Posner, B. Z. *The Leadership Challenge.* San Francisco: Jossey-Bass, 1987.

McCarthy, M. J. *Mastering the Information Age.* Los Angeles: Jeremy P. Tarcher, Inc., 1991.

McCune, S. "Restructuring Education: Context for World Action." *Educators Around the World Share Their Vision of a Design for School Year 2020.* Kansas City: Mid-Continent Regional Educational Laboratory, 1990, pp. 4-6.

McWhirt, R. A.; Reynolds, J. S.; and Achilles, C. M. "You Can't Cure It If You Don't Know You Have It." *National Forum of Applied Educational Research Journal* 2 (2): 35-41.

Mojkowski, C. *Developing Leaders for Restructuring Schools: New Habits of Mind and Heart.* Reston, Va.: National Association of Secondary School Principals, 1990.

Pascale, R. T. *Managing on the Edge: How the Smartest Companies Use Conflict To Stay Ahead.* New York: Simon & Schuster, 1990.

Peters, T., and Austin, N. *A Passion for Excellence.* New York: Warner Books, Inc., 1986.

Steinem, G. *Revolution from Within: A Book of Self-Esteem.* Boston: Little, Brown & Co., 1992.

Thomas, M. D. "Pluralism Gone Mad." *Phi Delta Kappa Educational Foundation,* 1981, pp. 19–29.

von Oech, R. *A Whack on the Side of the Head.* New York: Warner Books, Inc., 1983.

White, M. A. "Educating in the Information Age." *Educators Around the World Share Their Vision of a Design for School Year 2020.* Kansas City: Mid-Continent Regional Educational Laboratory, 1990, pp. 11–13.

# *Epilogue*

iving in a rapidly changing society requires the institutions that serve society change. This process of change has been fueled by the product of the educational process—the educated person. However, as the demands of the information society accelerate, the need for people who can gather and process information to create new knowledge in all walks of life is also accelerating. No longer can our schools merely offer students the opportunity to learn, we must ensure that *all* students do learn in order to become productive members of society.

Since education is a human enterprise, all members of the school community need to work in a collaborative manner with a primary focus on student learning outcomes and student learning conditions. As such, the schools, the administrators, and the teachers of the 21st century cannot be mass-produced in assembly-line fashion as they were in the industrial society. Rather, these schools must reflect and respond to the pluralistic needs of a multi-cultural and increasingly technological society. The characteristics of these schools must be described in terms that reflect growth and evolution. Their similarities must be engendered in their different interpretations of common themes. Nonetheless, if schools are to prepare students for the 21st century, all school community members must:

- ❦ Focus on the growth and development of all human capital in the school community, i.e., students, teachers, and administrators, and make the necessary changes to deliver services that meet the varied needs of people
- ❦ Internalize the belief that *all* students can learn, the expectation that students will learn if presented with the right learning opportunities, and the mental picture of everyone successfully progressing toward his or her full potential
- ❦ Recognize that the "one-best system" is the one that works best for an individual school, and that such a system may not be the best system for all schools
- ❦ Develop a school culture that nurtures the formation of cooperative networks of people to identify and address discrepancies between what is and what should be
- ❦ Promote and develop the leadership potential of people at all levels of the school system and within the school.

These activities must be undertaken at the school level with the active support of the school boards, central office, teacher unions, and with active participation from the public and private sectors, and community members, as well as those individuals who comprise the school community. If we are going to make the reforms to the educational process that have been suggested and if we are going to create a new future, we must collectively look to each situation and each problem as an opportunity to discover new and improved ways to best serve the needs and interests of students. They are our future.

As we began our odyssey the question was asked, can we get there from here? The time has now come to answer that question. As a result of the preceding questions, suggestions, and remarks from principals, the answer is both "yes" and "no." Yes, we can attain our vision for the future of education if we have the resolve to do so. On the other hand, the "no" response should not come as any great surprise. Since we recognize that nothing is as permanent as change, then each success should be viewed only as a temporary milestone along the road of our never-ending journey in search of excellence.

# Contributing Administrators

Theodore Arnold
Principal
Pinebrook Elementary School
Lincoln Park, N.J.

Jerome Auclair
Principal
Southington High School
Southington, Conn.

David Bergan
Principal
Milbank Senior High School
Milbank, S.Dak.

David E. Brown
Superintendent of Schools
Irvine Unified School District
Irvine, Calif.

Herb Bunch
Principal
9th Grade Building
New Castle, Ind.

Betty A. Calise
Principal
North Elementary School
Somerset, Mass.

Samuel H. Campbell
Principal
Franklin County Middle
    School
Rocky Mount, Va.

John Childs
Principal
Orem High School
Orem, Utah

Richard W. Cleveland
Principal
Battle Creek High School
Battle Creek, Nebr.

James A. Coles
Principal
Wootton High School
Rockville, Md.

Gary Crowell
Principal
Danbury High School
Danbury, Tex.

James M. Darland
Principal
East Central High School
Tulsa, Okla.

Robert A. DeRobbio
Principal (former)
Portsmouth High School
Portsmouth, R.I.

John D. Delaney
Principal
Parker Middle School
Reading, Mass.

Robert J. Drennen
Principal
Cherry Lane Elementary
    School
Sufferin, N.Y.

Roger Elford
Principal
Owosso High School
Owosso, Mich.

Robert V. Ericson
Principal
North High School
Sheboygan, Wis.

Sheryl Flowers
Principal
Metro Technical Vocational
    Area School
Oklahoma City, Okla.

Reginal R. Godin
Headmaster
Bellows Free Academy
St. Albans, Vt.

Andrew Henderson
Principal
Lincoln County High School
Lincolnton, Ga.

Donald G. Hovland
Principal
Stillwater Junior High School
Stillwater, Minn.

W. Duke Hucks
Principal
Hartville High School
Huntsville, S.C.

Ronald W. Jolley
Principal
Marsh Valley Middle School
Arimo, Idaho

Jaculine C. Jones
Principal
Sparks High School
Sparks, Nev.

David Kergaard
Principal
Kent County High School
Worton, Md.

William E. King
Principal
Rogers High School
Rogers, Ark.

Myron L. Liebrader
Principal
Grover Cleveland High
    School
Ridgewood, N.Y.

Jay F. Livziey
Principal
Roosevelt Middle School
Williamsport, Pa.

Patricia Lucas
Principal
Southeast High School
Bradenton, Fla.

John W. Mandernach
Principal
LeMars Junior High School
LeMars, Iowa

Joseph Matthews
Principal
Provo High School
Provo, Utah

Richard Niemeyer
Principal
Omak Senior High School
Omak, Wash.

Frederick P. Pasquariello
Principal
Nicholas A. Ferri Middle
    School
Johnston, R.I.

Douglas Pfeninger
Principal
Dartmouth Middle School
North Dartmouth, Mass.

Ross Poore
Principal
Central Davis Junior High
    School
Layton, Utah

Larry Roth
Principal
Adams Middle School
North Platte, Nebr.

Larry Schulz
Principal
Linderman School
Kalispell, Mont.

Robert Shamp
Principal
Findlay High School
Findlay, Ohio

Blair Slutz
Principal
West Holmes High School
Millersburg, Ohio

H. Dale Spaulding
Principal
Lampeter-Strasburg High
    School
Lampeter, Pa.

John Spradling
Principal
Park Junior High School
Artesia, N.Mex.

James Stenehjem
Assistant Principal
Grand Forks Central High
    School
Grand Forks, N.H.

Susan E. Simms
Principal
Pearl-Cohn Comprehensive
    High School
Nashville, Tenn.

Gerald Stinnett
Principal
Phoenix High School
Phoenix, Oreg.

Michael J. Thompson
Principal
Anaconda School District #10
Anaconda, Mont.

Joseph Wajtena
Principal
Champaign Central High
    School
Champaign, Ill.